The Best
Women's Monologues
of 1996

Other books by Jocelyn A. Beard

100 Men's Stage Monologues from the 1980s

100 Women's Stage Monologues from the 1980s

The Best Men's/Women's Stage Monologues of 1990

The Best Men's/Women's Stage Monologues of 1991

The Best Men's/Women's Stage Monologues of 1992

The Best Men's/Women's Stage Monologues of 1993

The Best Men's/Women's Stage Monologues of 1994

The Best Men's/Women's Stage Monologues of 1995

The Best Stage Scenes for Men from the 1980s

The Best Stage Scenes for Women from the 1980s

The Best Stage Scenes of 1992

The Best Stage Scenes of 1993

The Best Stage Scenes of 1994

The Best Stage Scenes of 1995

Monologues from Classic Plays 468 B.C. to 1960 A.D.

Scenes from Classic Plays 468 B.C. to 1970 A.D.

100 Great Monologues from the Renaissance Theatre

100 Great Monologues from the Neo-Classical Theatre

100 Great Monologues from the 19th C. Romantic & Realistic Theatres

The Best
Women's Monologues
of 1996

edited by Jocelyn A. Beard

MONOLOGUE AUDITION SERIES

A SMITH AND KRAUS BOOK

Published by Smith and Kraus, Inc.
One Main Street, Lyme, NH 03768

First Edition: October 1997
10 9 8 7 6 5 4 3 2 1

The Monologue Audition Series 1067-134X

NOTE: These monologues are intended to be used for audition and class study; permission is not required to use the material for those purposes. However, if there is a paid performance of any of the monologues included in this book, please refer to the permissions acknowledgment pages to locate the source who can grant permission for public performance.

Contents

Editor's Foreword

As a playwright, I know that crafting a good woman's monologue is a difficult thing. As an editor, I know that finding sixty good women's monologues for the Smith & Kraus annual collection will be a difficult, yet ultimately satisfying thing.

We women are devilishly complex characters; all too easy to over- or under-write for the stage. Too much fantasy, and she's a yutz…too much realism, and you've got another Jeanne D'Arc on your hands.

The problem is that although women have been speaking for thousands of years, not many have been listening to them. Modern, politically correct audiences of all genders are ready, willing, and rarin' to hear what women have to say, but all too often the finely honed female character on the stage suffers from the zeal of the playwright to create an omni-woman; a gal with enough estrogen *and* testosterone to sell a generation's worth of ideology in one two-hour encounter.

In reality, women live in and out of life's quiet moments. We're there in the delivery room, staring with disbelief at a child we suddenly know to be the one true love of our lives. We're there in the early mornings, preparing ourselves like tailored concubines for man's corporate realm in which we move like ghosts toward goals as empty as the hearts of those who limit our possibilities. No matter the place, no matter the time, we are there and we are ruled by one thing: love.

The monologues in this year's collection represent the best kind of writing for the stage. Unforgettable and real characters like Brian Friel's Molly Sweeny speak for all women in the quiet moments, reminding us that women like Hillary Clinton and

Oprah represent lives that are the exception rather than the rule. Issues like aging, infidelity, motherhood, and sexual orientation may seem like daytime talk fare, but they are the infrastructure of women's lives (just ask Hillary and Oprah!) and are well represented in this collection.

Women of generally acknowledged outrageous accomplishments are here as well. In Jeff Goode's hysterically dark *Portrait of the Virgin Mary Feeding the Dinosaurs* we encounter *the* Mary as she fusses through her laundry chores. Two former Bond girls enjoy a chance encounter in a Del-Mart in Toni Schlesinger's *James Bond's Old Girlfriends.* The lone survivor of a vicious serial killer struggles to raise her daughter and reconnect to life in Ludmilla Bollow's *The Church of the Holy Ghost.* Huge characters, quiet moments, lots of unconditional love.

This book will give you a fleeting taste of some of the finest plays of the season while introducing you to new characters who may offer a monologue that just might be the one you've been searching for. These women are real, and in the quiet moments of life they all shine.

Break a leg.

The Brickhouse
Patterson, NY
Summer 1997

This book is dedicated to Beth Bonnabeau Harding,
an unforgettable actress and good friend.

The Adjustment

Michael T. Folie

Scene: here and now

Dramatic
Sharon: a political lobbyist, Jewish, 40

> *Sharon has become attracted to her chiropractor, Dr. Matthew Cohen, who is a rather self-righteous Orthodox Jew. When she hears through the political grapevine that Matthew's rabbi cheated on his taxes, she takes great delight in telling him of his hero's misdeed. Matthew is unconvinced of the rabbi's guilt, however, and expresses his disapproval of Sharon's un-Orthodox lifestyle. Here, Sharon reacts to his insulting suggestions with anger.*

SHARON: *(To audience.)* I don't know why it got me so ticked off. I don't know why I cared at all. It just got me so mad, the idea of this grubby little Hasid Rabbi in his storefront temple thinking he was better than me. I mean, who are these guys anyway to judge somebody else? Look at how they treat their women. Matt's wife got pregnant again during the first month I was seeing him. Can you imagine?! They've already got two they don't know how they're going to take care of. And of course she can't work. Schimmel says women should just squeeze out one baby after another and make a kosher home and that's it. I look at those pathetic women pushing their strollers in the park, with those ugly wigs and those stockings with the thick seam running up the back, and I shudder and think "thank God! Just thank God I was born to normal, assimilationist parents." *(Pause.)* My mother's family came from Germany in 1938. She was fifteen. You know how they got out? My mother fucked the Nazi who issued the exit visas. She told me she had to do it three times. Once for each visa. She told me this when I was fifteen and she was dying of

1

breast cancer. She wanted my forgiveness. I said the only thing I couldn't forgive her for was not fucking him a few more times, get a few more Jews out. My mother was beautiful. But she always said her cousin Hannah was even more beautiful. After they left Germany, she wrote to Hannah from London, told her the name of the horny Nazi at the emigration office and gave her step-by-step instructions on how she could do the same thing while not getting pregnant. Ah, but Hannah's side of the family were religious nuts, like Schimmel. Like Matt. Her father got the letter and hit the ceiling. Wrote back and said my mother was a whore and he wanted nothing more to do with us. Well, good for him. He got his wish. He went up the chimney at Auschwitz, along with Hannah and everybody else on that side of the family.

Alphabet Of Flowers

Elyse Nass

Scene: a park bench

Dramatic
Jean: a woman confronting her first lover, 60

> *Jean and Kate were separated by Kate's parents when they were 20, and the young lovers made a vow to meet on the last day of September in their 60th year. Forty years later, their long-anticipated reunion is made uncomfortable by the memory of their youthful affair. Here, Jean tells Kate the difficult story of her life as a teacher in a small town.*

JEAN: In the late 50s, I decided I wanted to live in a small town...I found a teaching job in a small New England town. *(Pause.)* That's where I met Lynn. She taught in the school. I remember when I first saw her. I thought, this is the woman I'm going to spend the rest of my life with. She said, "Hello, my name is Lynn Day." I said, "What a beautiful name." And she had a beautiful smile. *(Pause.)* I'll fast forward now. We had a very nice life together, a very full life...teaching in the same school...even eating our lunch together. We had a lovely house...spent our summers traveling...Oh yes, there was so much to do...Check-ups, birthdays, holidays...and the laundry...Not necessarily in that order. We were always together. *(Pause.)* When we'd walk in the town, people would say, "Good morning, Miss Day, Miss Mills. Good evening, Miss Day, Miss Mills..." We were treated like two very respectable spinsters...We could always hear people under their breath..."What a shame those two never got married." We'd always smile back politely, acknowledging their greetings. To them, we were "those eccentrics" that never married. *(Pause.)* And twenty-three years passed by...in this slow, sing-song fashion...with "good morning, good evening, Miss Day, Miss

Mills…" *(Pause.)* Yes, this was the twentieth century in this hum-drum town. But despite its backwardness, it was a lovely place to behold…Full of trees and so green…One night, we took our usual walk, late at night to the lake. The moon was so full, the sky dotted with stars. We came here for years…But this time, for the first time we just held each other…ever so lightly…We never dared to make that slight gesture in public before…But now, after so many years…We did…Suddenly, from out of nowhere…a group of boys came at us from behind…punching us…beating us, and screaming at us, "You queers." Beating us, till blood was all over our bodies…They never took our money…No, they didn't want that…Just our lives…because of who we were. But I couldn't tell the police that. So I said we were robbed and beaten. *(Pause.)* Lynn got the worst of it. I never thought she'd stop bleeding. She had to be hospitalized. Every day I would visit her. I'd bring her baskets of flowers. Every kind of flower imaginable, from anemones to zinnias…an alphabet of flowers. I was hoping the flowers would revive her, make her see all the beauty in living…She was never quite the same after the beating. You see, her wounds healed. But her spirit was dead. In the town she grew up and loved…to be beaten like that. She began to drink. And several months later, she had an accident. Her car went off the road. *(Pause.)* After she died, I couldn't keep the truth in any longer. Several weeks later, I went to the police. This time I decided to tell them everything. When they saw me, they said, "What a shame about Miss Day, but she shouldn't have been drinking and driving." And then I said, "She started drinking because this whole town drove her to it." And then I said, "Remember the terrible beatings we both got a few months ago?" And they said, "The one where you both were robbed and beaten?" I said, "No, we were never robbed." And they shouted, "You told us you were robbed!" "Yes, I did," I said. "But I lied. I was afraid to tell you what really happened. But now it doesn't matter. We were beaten. Beaten because we had been lovers." And their faces swelled up with such an ugliness, with such a rage…looking at me in this totally, horrified unbelieving

4

way…And I said proudly, "Lynn and I were lovers for twenty-three years." And there was this hateful silence. I left…Then the story went around…about us. Now those same people that had been saying, "So sorry to hear about Miss Day…" were now whispering terrible things…Their faces seething with a terrible anger…No more polite, nodding faces…Just hatred in their eyes. Although these people never said one word, mind you…their faces would say everything…They would look at me with such horror… and then all that whispering…I couldn't teach in the school. I had to leave. So I came back to the city where I grew up…to start again.

Ask Nostradamus

R. J. Marx

Scene: 16th century France

Comedic
Anne de Jumelle: wife of the famous seer, 20–30

> *Being the wife of a prophet can be quite difficult as Anne here reveals.*

ANNE: When are you going to get a job, a real job?

[MICHEL: I want to prophesy! I like to prophesy!]

ANNE: Prophesy, forget it. Talk about a nowhere job. Look at Jean-Claude, a tanner. Gaultier, a designer. And what do I tell the girls about you, Michel? A seer? visionary? A no-good worthless dropout who couldn't write fortune cookies for a condemned Chinese Restaurant. Speaking of which, when was the last time you took me out to dinner? Huh? And I'm not talking about one of those fast food drive-ins, either. We gotta eat every goddamn meal in, and y'know what take out's like around here? Now see this, M. de Notredame, soon to be known to the world as Nostradamus! Get your act together, visions or no vision, or I'm calling it quits. Got it, buster?

The Batting Cage

Joan Ackerman

Scene: a hotel room in Florida

Serio-Comic
Julianna: a woman vacationing with her sister, 40

> *Julianna and Wilson have journeyed to St. Augustine, Florida,*
> *at the request of Morgan, Wilson's twin sister who has been*
> *dead for two years. Wilson has been uncommunicative with*
> *Julianna since Morgan's death, withdrawing into a state of*
> *functional catatonia. Julianna has tried to deal with her grief*
> *in a more proactive manner as she here describes.*

JULIANNA: I haven't mentioned this to mother but I've been receiving some acupuncture lately from a beginner acupuncturist, at a discount because he's in need of accumulating hours. For a minor medical condition, minor, don't be too concerned. I can't explain it all now but the basic theory is that the cause of illness has to do with an imbalance of the five elements that make up ch'i: wood, fire, earth, metal, water, and one way for them to diagnose which element is out of balance is by color, what color do you feel very strongly about, love or detest. First he thought I had a fire imbalance, someone who is cold physically and emotionally, as in one's fire is out, feeling parched and arid in mind, body, spirit. The color that corresponds with fire is red. Well, I didn't think that was right, I wasn't feeling passionate about red either way. I'm not going to wear this dress, I look like I should be offering people cheese samples on a large corning ware plate in a supermarket. *(After studying herself in a full-length mirror, she pulls off that dress and starts assembling another outfit, perhaps a blouse and a print skirt.)* Then he thought maybe I had an earth imbalance which has to do with the intake of nourishment and getting nourished, or not, lacking the ability to create roots for oneself, easily pushed over, that seemed more like it. I certainly have not been feeling particularly nourished lately, but then there was all this implication about having difficulty with sterility I told him it was my husband who had that problem not me. Anyway, the color for an earth imbalance is yellow. *(Not satisfied, she unbuttons the blouse and hangs it up. Reaches for another one.)* Then I read about water and I was sure I had a water imbalance, meanwhile all along he's taking my pulses, sticking needles in me as though it's earth. The organs associated with water are the kidneys and the bladder and you know I have the bladder of a grasshopper. The flavor that corresponds to water is salty, me, Mrs. Ruffles potato chip, the sense organ governed by the water element is the ears, my hearing is painfully acute, the color blue. Well, my car is blue. Is this me? I think not. *(Studies herself in the mirror, takes off the blouse and the skirt. Stares at the closet. During the following puts on another outfit and takes it off.)* It was disconcerting. Not to be sure which element was out of balance and having him treating me perhaps making it all worse. Well, the emotion corresponding to metal is grief, and I've suffered my share of that recently. The sound corresponding to metal is weeping, God knows I have wept these past two years and dreams associated with metal are of cruel killing of people, I've had those. The color is white. Well? Any thoughts? You know one thing, Wilson, about living alone now, ever since Carl moved out, I find myself speaking out loud. I'll find myself in the kitchen talking with no one there. I feel like a loon. I'm thinking about getting a cat or a goldfish, just to have a target to aim my voice at. At least now, here, *you're* listening. I'm not just ranting and raving to myself. Wilson?

Burning Down The House

Jocelyn Beard

Scene: a farmhouse in Provence, France

Serio-Comic
Claudia: a woman on the verge of self-discovery, 40s

> *Claudia has been struggling to make her life make sense for quite some time. Now on holiday in the south of France with her best friend, Heddy, she seems ready to confront the demons she's thus far avoided so neatly. When a younger Frenchman, Alex, asks her out on a date, she accepts without considering the consequences. Here, she expresses her feelings of loneliness and alienation to Heddy, who has passed out from a combination of Xanax, red wine, and jet lag.*

CLAUDIA: *(To herself.)* Unbelievable! I've been in France less than six hours and I have a date with a tall handsome Frenchman who thinks my name is enchanting. Correction: I have a date with a tall, handsome and significantly *younger* Frenchman who *says* he thinks my name is enchanting. Who could have predicted such a thing? Could you have predicted that, Heddy? You seem to know so much about my life. *(Seeing her.)* Ahh, I see you've managed to rediscover the position that you were most likely to be found in during freshman year at Hofstra. Don't move. *(Claudia retrieves one of her bags and fishes out her camera. As she studies Heddy through the viewfinder.)* Now this brings back memories, my dear. Memories of the good old days before you got a job and I became a "hausfrau." I just love it when you call me that, you know. Just love it. I suppose you'll kill me for taking this, but, too bad. Mark will get a big kick out of it. *(She takes the shot. Heddy makes an impolite noise of some kind.)* Enchanting. *(Claudia rises and crosses to the window.)* Just listen to that wind. It's…it's…the most incredible thing I've ever heard! It sounds like…I don't know…some kind of primitive force that's trying to smash right through into this world from…a place of dark dreams. *(A pause.)* Very dark dreams. *(A pause.)* Mistral. Such a beautiful name. I wonder what it means? *(She listens to the Mistral for a moment.)* You know, Heddy, I think that if I stood out there long enough, in the Mistral, that eventually my mind would be blown clear. All my thoughts, all my notions, all my feelings and all my memories would be blown clean away to Africa, where they'd turn into Sahara dust. Then the wicked jumble of my life would finally *finally* cease to be. Wouldn't that be wonderful, Heddy? To be able to start again? No memories, no lingering images tucked away somewhere in between synapses. Just a brilliant, clean mind. Like a person with amnesia. God, that would be wonderful: to be so empty. *(She listens to the Mistral and then turns back to Heddy with a smile.)* Now there's a topic that Ricki and Sally Jesse haven't covered. "Today we're talking to Middle-Aged Women Who Hate Their Lives So Much They'd Do Anything Including Self-Induced Amnesia To Start Over Again!" Would you finally respect me then? If I went on Ricki and confessed to the world via the cathode ray what I'll never be able to confess to you…or to myself? Probably not. Better just to become empty. It works for the Taoists. *(Looking out the window.)* I wish you could see these colors. The sky is almost carnelian, can you imagine? Carnelian.

Burning Down The House

Jocelyn Beard

Scene: a farmhouse in Provence, France

Dramatic
Claudia: a woman on the verge of self-discovery, 40s

> *While on holiday in the south of France, Claudia falls in love
> with Alex, a younger man whose wife was killed by a sniper
> in Sarajevo. When she accidentally causes a fire that burns
> down the house once inhabited by Alex and his wife, Claudia
> flees to a nearby lavender field where she hopes to be able
> to collect her thoughts. Here she is discovered by Alex's sis-
> ter, Juliette, to whom she explains the reasons why she isn't
> ready for a relationship.*

CLAUDIA: Juliette, my life is such a ridiculous mess right now that
I'm not fit to be pursuing a relationship with anyone—let alone a
younger man who doesn't even live in the same country as I do
whose house I just burned down!

[JULIETTE: In what way is your life messy?]

CLAUDIA: Well, for starters, my marriage of some eighteen years is
a total sham. The only relationship I've ever had with anyone—
except with Jess, my daughter—that means anything to me is
totally fucked. Don't get me wrong, I love Jessica more than my
own heart, but she's sixteen. In a few more years, she'll be gone.
What will I have then? I have no career, to speak of. No friends
who I can trust or who can trust me. No one to love. I don't even
have a god damn dog. What I do have is the biggest house in
Cathedral Park, a two-thousand-square-foot condo in Boca
Raton, I drive a Lincoln Town Car…Jesus! I've surrounded myself
with so much empty space that even if I start walking right now,
I'll never get to the door. Never. No matter how fast I walk, or
even if I run it won't matter. I will have nothing.

The Church Of The Holy Ghost

Ludmilla Bollow

Scene: a wooden church

Dramatic
Erin: a woman tortured by memories of the past and fears of the future, 30s

> *The sole survivor of a vicious serial killer, Erin has spent the years battling to hold onto her daughter, who was conceived during her capture. Here, Erin finally tells her terrifying and heartbreaking story to a caring friend.*

ERIN: *(Sits quietly for moment. Then begins breathing heavily. Speaks in short gasps.)* I—I was walking home alone. I heard foot-steps, behind me. I went faster. He went faster… *(Stops.)*

[JERICO: Then what?]

ERIN: He—he grabbed me from behind—so tight—I couldn't breathe. A knife at my throat. I couldn't even scream—make any sound. He put this bag over my head—tied my hands, feet—shoved me into the trunk of his car. *(Pause.)*

[JERICO: Take your time.]

ERIN: *(As if there, reliving.)* When he took the bag off—I was in this farm building. A concrete room. Women in chains, against the walls, everywhere. He tied me with ropes and he did things to me—horrible things. Poured liquids in every opening of my body. I finally passed out…When I woke up, it was quiet. My skin still slippery—from the liquids. I rubbed my wrists raw, somehow, slipped out of the ropes. One woman pointed, she couldn't even talk—to a small door in the bottom of the huge locked door, where they shoved food in. I slid through. Ran, naked, bleeding—

> *(Anguished cries rise up from her depths as she goes into a slight faint.)*

[JERICO: Just relax now. It's all over, all cried out.]

ERIN: *(Reviving.)* They found me. I don't remember that part. Just waking up in a hospital bed and screaming over and over about that place—the women still there.

[JERICO: Finish later.]

ERIN: It never finishes.

[JERICO: Do it now then.]

ERIN: …They caught him. Found the other women too. All dead by then. Starved. Tortured. I was the only one alive to testify. It was months before the trial… *(Pause.)* Once I knew I was pregnant, I wanted to tear it out of me. Every memory of that horrible night… *(Different tone.)* I went to this clinic. They strapped me to this table. Strong hands holding me down. My body began quivering. This masked doctor's face, coming closer. "We're going to vacuum it out of you—" "No!" I didn't want anything entering my body again. I let out this terrifying scream, that wailed away into a continuous faraway sound—the faint cry of a newborn baby. I closed my eyes as tight as I could, but all I could see was this beam of light—a pinpoint of brightness piercing through all the deep dark. Every instinct within me clawed to protect this one spark of light, because if I let it go out—everything would become total darkness again. Saving this speck of life was the only hope of saving myself. I screamed and screamed and broke loose. And I escaped—just like the time before…

[JERICO: *(Takes her hand.)* I cry in my heart for everything's that's happened to you.]

ERIN: *(Jerks her hand away.)* I fought my mother—I fought everybody—to keep this child. I had always wanted a baby and this might be my only chance…I knew I'd never have sex again.

Dance With Me

Stephen Temperley

Scene: here and now

Serio-Comic
Sally: a woman fighting her addiction to love, 30s

> *Sally has finally given the boot to Jack and Talbot, two men who have taken turns using her. Here, she describes her first moment without a man in her life.*

SALLY: You know when it hit me? When I got home and the place was empty. That's when I realized what I'd done. I closed the door and sat in the hall but I wouldn't let myself panic. I'm breathing deeply; I've got to stay calm; I can't go to pieces now. I'm used to them, that's all it is. I'm used to having them around. *(She pushes the men away. They exit. She stands to survey the room.)* Look at my place; look at all my things; my books; my desk. Talbot's stuff I'll put by the door. He can get it when I'm not here. I'll take yoga. I'll practice relaxation. I'll do aerobics. I'll take it one day at a time. *(As she speaks, she changes her clothes. Beginning in a pair of sweatpants and a sweater of Jack's, she ends in a smart, tailored suit.)* The first day I notice there's no more rage, no more tears, no more falling short of Jack's expectations. Day two: no more phone calls at the office, no more little jokes, complaints, reminders, tips. Day three:; I'm feeling better; I'm feeling okay. I called my friends; I called a shrink. No more making do with what I don't want; no more guessing which way he wants me to jump and always guessing wrong. No more having him there when I get home late and I haven't called and he's all upset. But I know he loves me. Think he loves me. Day ten, eleven, twelve, two weeks; it's been two weeks and every day in every way I'm getting better and better. I avoid restaurants. *(She removes her sweatpants and pulls on a skirt.)* No more waiting for him to change or me to change or something to change; no more terror he'll leave me one day because I already left him. *(She steps into her shoes.)* Two months now and I'm doing fine. I left my shrink; the hell with him, too. I'm redoing the apartment. I bought new plants. Talbot let the others die. Sometimes I get a bit short of breath but I'm hanging on. No more loving him; no more wearing his clothes. *(She removes Jack's sweater.)* No more making allowances. No more *Jeopardy,* no more *Court TV,* no more *Masterpiece Theatre.* No more worrying he's losing his hair— though it seems to be spreading on his shoulders. No more crying in the bathroom because he's sleeping with my friends. *(She puts on her jacket, earrings, etc.)* I called Annie today; we might have lunch. I have to go in a restaurant sometime. Five months now and I'm being promoted. My own department; my own staff; eight brokers working under me, five of them men; they call me "Boss." *(She shakes out her hair and sits, sleek and poised.)* I'm not going to cry. Hints of a partnership are in the air.

Detail Of A Larger Work

Lisa Dillman

Scene: San Miguel Allende, Guanajuanto, Mexico

Dramatic
Vanessa: elegant and graceful, the wife of a great painter, 63

> *Vanessa and Ed live in Mexico where they are paid a visit by a young photographer and his girlfriend, Chloe. Here, Vanessa tells Chloe the unhappy story of her first husband's death.*

VANESSA: Oh. He didn't *die* of cancer.

[CHLOE: *(Finally, almost against her will.)* What happened?]

VANESSA: Oh. We were living in Evanston, Illinois. Mac taught first-year French at Northwestern. He took his cancer treatments at the university hospital—it had a very fine medical center. I remember he had his treatments every Thursday morning. The doctors had told him there wasn't much hope. He refused to believe them. *(Beat.)* The house we lived in was made of stone and looked like a woodcutter's cottage straight out of a child's storybook. It had a massive fireplace in the front room and little windows that opened out like doors. It was a magical sort of place. The neighborhood was full of trees. And children. And old people. Everyone knew everyone. It used to be like that, it really did, people used to know their neighbors. *(Suddenly self-conscious, she mimes a cane and cackles in an imitation of an ancient crone.)* He had just left for his treatment. I was in the front room in just my slip. Blowing kisses through the window. He was standing on the curb, pretending that each kiss was hitting him in the jaw or the eye like this. *(Mimes.)* Clowning, you know, like he did. He stepped off the curb backwards and was doing that old Groucho Marx walk across the street. And a blue Buick came along right then and hit him just as hard as you can possibly imagine.

[CHLOE: Oh!]

VANESSA: It happened so *fast*. It seemed like some kind of continuation of Mac's little routine. Keystone Kops or something. Anyway, there was Mac lying in the street and there was the blue Buick, stopped a little way up the block. But after it sat there a second, it sped off down the road. I suppose the screech of the tires was what brought me out of my trance. I ran to the front door, but it was locked—Mac always took such care to lock the door when he left me alone—and I honestly couldn't make my hand understand the lock mechanism. Nothing made sense to me. *(Laughs.)* Do you ever do that?

[CHLOE: Do what?]

VANESSA: Oh, focus on details as a way of avoiding the whole picture? It occurs to me now that I felt safe as long as I was inside that house. As long as I couldn't get the door open, Mac wasn't really out there bleeding in the…When I finally got to him, Mac had this look on his face—as if he'd just walked into a surprise party. He was so thin, you know, from the cancer and all the treatments. His eyes were just enormous. He couldn't see me, couldn't hear me. There was blood coming from his ears and the corners of his mouth. He said, "I'm here. I'm *here.*" I've always wondered about that. I'm here. Plaintive, you know. As if he thought he might be left behind. And then…that was all. Like shutting off a light. *(Beat.)* Oh, listen to me. My whole life story, as if you asked. Would you like to have a little drinkie-poo?

Detail Of A Larger Work

Lisa Dillman

Scene: San Miguel Allende, Guanajuanto, Mexico

Dramatic
Chloe: a young woman with a terrible secret, 20s

> *Chloe and Zach have traveled to this part of Mexico to visit*
> *Vanessa and Ed, who were close friends of Duane, a man*
> *who allowed Zach to chronicle his slow death from AIDS in*
> *photographs. Unknown to Ed and Vanessa, Chloe could no*
> *longer bear Duane's suffering, and smothered him with a pil-*
> *low. When this secret is revealed, Vanessa is horrified and*
> *demands that Chloe and Zach leave immediately. Here, Chloe*
> *attempts to leave Vanessa with a happier memory of her dear*
> *friend.*

CHLOE: He used to tell me stories about you sometimes. *(Vanessa looks at her.)* You and Ed had a house outside Boston. A Cape Cod. With a yard like a meadow. Rolling and green. And an old-fashioned wishing well. You and Duane stood at that well one night and tossed in wishes until you were both completely hoarse.

[VANESSA: Duane had brought…eight rolls of pennies that time.]

CHLOE: And the next morning, Duane awoke there in the attic where he liked to sleep whenever he stayed with you; remember? His bed right under the eaves. The little tiny dormer windows. It wasn't even six A.M., but the sun was up and the air was so clear. Sparkling. Swept all the way clean. He put on his robe and crept down the stairs. *(Vanessa leans forward, listening.)* The house was still in shadow and very quiet. He moved through like a cat so as not to wake you and Ed. When he got to the kitchen, he saw that the back door was open, and through the screen door, he could see you. Your back to him, with the sunshine like a halo over your head. So still. Listening to the birds, watching the incredible morning around you. He was afraid to move—afraid to spoil that completely perfect moment. He stood there for a long, long time. And finally. Slowly. You turned your head, as if you'd known he was there from the beginning. And you said, "I take back all those wishes, Duane. This morning I see…I have everything."

[VANESSA: Duane told you all that.]

CHLOE: Then the two of you sat there and talked, hand in hand like a couple of young lovers. And laughed. And told each other secrets that would always be kept. He could tell you anything, he said. You never judged him *(Beat.)* I didn't know him the way you did, Vanessa. But I knew him at a time when you didn't. He couldn't…stand any more suffering. At the end. He wasn't a person anymore. He was just nerve endings and inflammation and…I think you know all this anyway.

Doppleganger

Jo J. Adamson

Scene: the deck of a cruise ship

Serio-Comic
Young Woman: a passenger on a cruise ship, 20s

> *When the ship's photographer offers to take her picture, the young woman ruminates on her appearance.*

YOUNG WOMAN:
A thousand things go through my head as the photographer
checks the light. Is my lipstick glossy? Cheeks luminous?
Figure voluptuous. Eyes bright, teeth pearly? Hair,
curly? Will I project the correct image.

Young girl Vacationing? Young Miss Contemplating? Ingenue
  Visits Atlanta.
Society Deb. On Verandah. Young Beauty Soaks Up Sun.
  American Miss
Visits Venice. Austrian Lass Studies Sunset. Fraulein Heinler
  Smiles At
Photographer. Mademoiselle Cline Boards Luxury Liner.

(Photographer continues to check equipment. Woman powders her nose.)

Focus your lens on my tight skin
I was born for the close-up
The sun is my friend: I open like a flower
Count compliments that blossom in the
summer of my hours

(Photographer continues to check equipment, takes light readings, etc.)

Come to me. Come on. Photograph the light around my
cells. The shadow of my smile. Soft focus me to the
edge of eternity. I'm the infinite closing of your
iris shot. The particle in your eye that won't wash out.

Feel me to the whorls of your fingers
Preserve the dream emulsion in your soul
Embalm the Celluloid daylights out of me and
I'll look good in tomorrow's photogravure.

(Woman assumes different model poses.)

How do you want me?
It's a rhetorical question.
Fetching?, perhaps
Whimsical, capricious, coquettish to be sure
Here's Pert, Saucy, Bewitching...Alluring
I give you, Tantalizing, Teasing, Tempting, always.

I am by instinct.
Toss of head, angle of chin, curve of neck
Always right
up to the orgasmic dissolve.

(Woman addresses photographer.)

We work well together
Where do you stop and I begin?
I wait your separation
in safe-light suspension.

O.K., I'm ready
Click the shutter

(Woman becomes flustered, unsure.)

I'm all a flutter
You'd think I'd be used to this

Each time is like the first virgin thrust
One more minute,
My makeup's running, nose shiny…
No!, I'm beauty's perfection
The stuff dreams are made of
"No sweat" as they say,
Click the shutter while the feeling rises
Take the wave at its crest

Now!, fire when ready, Sir
I'm at my best.

Doppleganger

Jo J. Adamson

Scene: the deck of a cruise ship

Serio-Comic
Old Woman: passenger on a cruise ship, 60–70

> *Here, an older woman speaks of her newly discovered love of reading.*

OLD WOMAN: The sun is healing.
Its ultraviolet assuages the aches;
I bask in its friendly wake
    (Wryly.)
A five billion year old deep-heat massage
    (Old Woman refers to book.)
I read a good deal.
It's only been in the winter of my life
that fact has been ignored
Books are conversation bridges when the hand
that turns the page
are not speckled with age
    (Dryly.)
For those of you eaten by curiosity,
It's Walpole I read
Sketches of London, brilliant in detail
Stories of court, Lords and Commons

He suffered agonies from gout
I do as well

"The world," Walpole writes,
"Is a comedy for those who think,
and a tragedy for those who feel."

*(Woman ponders this. Closes book, and reaches under her lap
robe for cigarette. Puts it in cigarette holder and lights up.)*
I believe I will.
There is much pleasure in the printed word,
I mull over incubated thoughts. Hatch them
at leisure
A contrast, indeed
to ship deck talks that assail me daily

(Woman touches book.)

These thoughts?
I don't let them out of my head until I'm good and ready

(She smokes for a moment in silence and then says:)

I'm an old vampire
Cast no reflection in the dark pupil of the public's eye
My nourishment is the hot blood of literary people
fallen empires

They say we're in the last days of Pompeii
Perhaps we are;
couldn't care either way
I die from day to day

The Ends Of The Earth

David Lan

Scene: a hospital sitting room

Dramatic
Cathy: a woman torn apart by her daughter's terminal illness and her failing marriage, 30s

> *When Cathy fears her husband, Daniel, is near to a complete breakdown, she leaves her terminally ill daughter to visit him in the Balkans where he has been working as a geologist on a dam project. Daniel informs Cathy that he hates her for their daughter's illness and then leaves her in the tiny village to go seek out a wise man who is rumored to have the power to cure the sick. Back in London, Cathy reveals to Daniel what she did when left alone in the village.*

CATHY: Oh, what a baby. *(She moves away.)*

[DANIEL: (Wailing.) Why are you leaving me?]

CATHY: Because I'd rather sit over here, that's why. You believe you understood something there, do you? You saw into things? Do you remember that musician?

[DANIEL: Which one?]

CATHY: I thought he was good looking. You called him a brute.

[DANIEL: No, that was the waiter, the manager.]

CATHY: Was it? Anyway...I mean the one who took you up the mountain. What I wanted to tell you was...You insisted on going up the mountain. I'd left Sally. You left me. I was so alone. *(She is crying.)* I went to bed with him

[DANIEL: Did you?]

CATHY: You had to go! So go, damn you. Ten minutes went by, he sauntered in. Why did I do it? Did I want to? You say we should do what we want.

[DANIEL: Did I?]

CATHY: What we feel. So I did. I thought, any second you'd come in. Was I hoping you would? That would show you. What? Many things. That it wasn't only you who can choose what to do. So I did it. *(Silence.)* It wasn't very nice actually. I wouldn't have said God was in him. You reminded me of it when you talked about masturbating. It felt as if that's all he was doing. Using me as a fist. You're right. I didn't fancy him. Funny, you always remember men more clearly than I do. But I was so angry. With you. So what do you think? Was 'God' in there? Or was that simply a bad thing to do? *(Silence.)* Because that's how I am, you see. Bad. And you know what I feel? Shall I tell you why I feel Sally was born ill? I know what I'm going to say isn't true but it is true. There's something bad in me. And it came out. And it got into her. I love her so much but somehow it came out of me. And though we say she's better and the doctors do, we know she's only better than she was. She could get worse. Most likely she will. Most likely she'll die. And that's because not all the badness has come out of me. There's more. And all the time it gets bigger and bigger, it grows and grows. What does it feed on? Shall I tell you what I think? It feeds on my loathing. Of you. Because I do loathe you. Your weakness. So you see, you have to leave, you have to. I want you to leave. Do you hear me? I want you to leave us, Sally and me. I want you to go. Oh God, go. I do. Please. I don't believe any of this, what I've said. I don't believe it but I believe. So go. Now. Please. Please.

Fragments

John Jay Garrett

Scene: events throughout the life and death of Jack Wilson

Dramatic
Maureen: Jack's mother, 20s

> *Here, the determined young Maureen frets over her sick baby. It is 1949. A soft light falls on Maureen Wilson, rocking gently in a large wooden rocking chair. She is wearing a heavy white nightgown and cradles a small bundle. There is a lamp and an end table with a small bowl next to her. As she sings she dips a small rag in the bowl, rings it out, and wipes down the baby. Although she is upset, there is a placid calm to her.*

Fais dodo, Colas mon p'tit frere,
Fais dodo, t'auras du lolo.
Maman est en haut,
Qui fad un Gateau,
Papa est en bas,
Qui fad du chocolate
Fais dodo, Colas mon p'tit frere,
Fais dodo, t'auras du folo.

MAUREEN: (Sleep now, Nicolas my little brother.) (Sleep now, there are those who care.) (Mama is upstairs.) (Ready with your milk.) (Papa is in the kitchen.) (Ready with some chocolate.) (Sleep now, Nicolas my little brother.) (Sleep now, there are those who care.)

Oh God you're burning up. I'm not ready for this Jack. What else can I do for you? I hate it when people talk to babies and ask questions. Okay listen, I know you're not going to answer me, but I'm just so scared. Why aren't you crying? You're sick Jack.

Sick babies are supposed to cry, aren't they? Maybe Daddy knows. What am I saying, Daddy can't even keep fish. Just don't start convulsing on me. Promise me that. Doctor Kameny said as long as you don't go into convulsions, you'll be okay. Did you hear that? No. convulsions. I know that's kind of a big word, but we're both going to have to learn fast here. Fais dodo, Colas mon p'tit frere, Fais dodo, t'auras du lolo. Maman est en haut, Qui fait un Gateau...Come on Brad, hurry up. I wish Maman was still alive. She would have loved you... God, please. Jack? Daddy's going to be home from work soon. We have... *(The light flickers and goes out. Bulb's dead. The darkness is total at first, but a soft blue light helps our eyes adjust.)* Okay, now that pisses me off. God, I swear to you, if you do anything to this baby...I know they say in church that it all happens because you make it that way and it's all part of a plan. As far as I'm concerned right here and now that's all so much bullshit. Sorry Jack. If it all just happens, then it happens. But if you take him because you've got it worked up as some piece in a puzzle, then I swear I'll hate you forever. I don't care what good you think it's for, I'll hate you. That may not mean much to you, but it does to me. I know I haven't talked to you since Mom died but...aghh, I sound like a... *(Jack starts crying. Hiccups at first, but building into a full-fledged baby cry.)* Yes, Jack. Good boy. Keep talking to me. *(The sound of a car engine shutting off and a door slamming.)* I think that's Daddy. Everything's gonna be fine now. Daddy's gonna take us to the doctor. I know Jack. I know. Mommy's here. Mommy'll take care of you. I promise.

Fragments

John Jay Garrett

Scene: events throughout the life and death of Jack Wilson

Dramatic
Maureen: Jack's mother, 40s

> *Some twenty years later, Maureen recalls finding out that Jack was killed in Vietnam.*

MAUREEN: I told myself I wasn't going to talk at this meeting, but I guess I always say that. I just wanted to respond to Janet's question. No Janet, not at all. I remember I used to sit at the kitchen table and stare at the door for what seemed like hours, waiting for the doorbell to ring. Sometimes, I'd even stand at the front window, expecting a government car to pull up. And it seemed that every time the doorbell would ring, I had forgotten to expect it. My heart would go all fluttery on me and I'd hate myself for not being prepared. I used to pore over his letters for days, looking for every clue into his life there, what sort of changes it was forcing upon him. I remember he would sometimes tell me about KIA's and WIA's and I almost fooled myself into thinking it was like his high school soccer scores. *(Smiles.)* I guess you know what I mean. And all that was before my husband found me in line at the DMV and told me Jack was dead. One of the first things I started to do after I found out was go to the airport. I started going three times a week, sometimes four. I used to stand there with a small flag, not because I believed in the war, or the government, but just so the boys coming home knew someone back here cared about them coming home alive, mourned for what they had gone through. I was arrested once when I punched a girl who had just spat on one of them. Knocked her right in the nose. I felt like a real jerk afterward. Here I am, a forty-three-year-old woman, hitting some kid who doesn't really know what she's doing. But it just made me so mad when I saw the look on that poor boy's face. I kept going to the airport until seventy-three. Sometimes I'd tell them that I loved them, or give them a hug, but mostly I just…mostly I just imagined that I was waiting for Jack. *(Pause.)* No Janet, I don't believe you think about him too much. I believe everyone else thinks about them too little.

A Girl's Tie To Her Father

Sari Bodi

Scene: here and now

Serio-Comic
June: an alcoholic mom with a wry sense of humor, 40s

> *Because of June's drinking, her daughter Claire has been removed from her care several times. Here, the philosophical booze hound addresses Claire's concerned teacher.*

JUNE: Hello, Mrs. McKnight. I'm Eclaire's mother. Oh yes, that's Claire's real name, named after my food cravings during my pregnancy. Oh here, I promised you my recipe for the perfect martini. Three ounces of Bombay Sapphire gin. A splash of vermouth. Three green olives. Cheers. Now I ask you, if God hadn't meant for us to drink, would she have invented fermentation? Oh, you liked that martini? I discovered them at Malcolm's. After Claire's conception, Malcolm handed me a martini, and said, "Here, now you can experience Dionysus every day of your life." Oh, you've been to Malcolm's? When you were younger, and still believed in changing your luck. I've since discovered that luck is just luck, contrary to what the self-help books tell us about making our own. Someone sitting at a luncheon counter in Hollywood with her perky breasts nicely ensconced in a tight sweater is going to catch the eye of a talent scout, and someone else who has equally perky breasts who was supposed to go to that same luncheonette, missed her bus, and got there a half hour later. That woman ate her lunch and left, but the other woman, the movie star, has been dining out for the rest of her life. Because luck is luck. And that's why they invented psychiatry—to allow the unlucky to find justification for their unluckiness. Cheers.

Grace

Albert Verdesca

Scene: a cemetery

Dramatic
Orrine: a woman trying to make peace with her past, 30s

Here, Orrine visits her mother's grave on her birthday and does her best to put to rest the demons that haunt her memory.

ORRINE: Happy birthday, Grace. *(She sips the champagne and giggles.)* It's such a beautiful day for a birthday party, so bright and sunny. I brought you some flowers, foxglove, your favorite, and some begonias. I know how much you like begonias. *(Pause.)* I guess you thought you'd never see me again after all that happened. To be honest with you, I didn't know if I really wanted to see you. *(Pause.)* I brought lunch. I don't like drinking on an empty stomach. Not like the old days. Grace? *(She takes out food and utensils and eats and drinks throughout.)* Remember the time we took those trail horses up the state park lookout and picnicked with that great view of the mountains surrounding us. God—we got so shit-faced on champagne that day we could hardly get back on the horses. We both threw our guts up on the ride back down. Remember that day? *(Pause.)* I don't get drunk anymore. Not because I'm sorry what happened. Just learned to temper my drinking after ten years sober. Can you believe that Grace? Ten years. No liquor consumption allowed up at Birchbrook. It wasn't easy at first but you kinda get used to it. *(Pause.)* I brought curry chicken salad with walnuts. Haven't had curry in such a spell. You never did develop a taste for it—and real champagne from France, not like all that cheap fizz we used to drink back then. *(She drinks some and giggles.)* Funny, how the bubbles always made me giggle. *(She eats some salad.)* Oh, look! A chipmunk. Haven't seen a chipmunk in a years. Never really appreciated them in the past but just look at them now—one of God's little creatures. Wonder what they think of when they scurry around like that? *(She makes a kissing sound to the chipmunk and throws a walnut to it.)* Do you think chipmunks like curried walnuts? *(She laughs then continues eating.)* I've been pretty lonely these past few years—not that we were ever very close. Even those times when we poured our hearts out to each other, when we were drunk, it was always the alcohol did the talking. Never the same the next day. Hardly spoke to each other at all, some days. Guess it'd be just the same now if it weren't for the accident. I try not to think about it. Funny thing is I can't help *but* think about it. It's become a constant presence in my thoughts and dreams. *(She eats.)* Mmm, this chicken is mighty tasty. I just love the combination of chicken and nuts. Why, I can remember granddaddy bringing out two large, wooden bowls after Thanksgiving dinner. One filled with fruit and the other with nuts. Remember? Jesus, lord, I was so young then. Little children are God's greatest gifts—so delicate and innocent—so precious, like that little chipmunk running around, and then we grow up. Where is that moment in time, that place, where the evanescence of youth gives way to the encroachment of maturity, when the only bubbles that make us giggle anymore are found inside a bottle of champagne. I suppose life changes us all. Yet some people never lose their childlike innocence. I'd love to know how they do that, short of flying off with Peter Pan. *(She laughs. Pause.)* I didn't bring a birthday cake, Grace. I didn't think it was necessary, seeing how you always hated cake except if it was laced with bourbon. I'm sure you won't miss it. *(Pause. She continues eating.)* Now I know you're not going to take too kindly to this Grace, but Dr. Rosenberg—that's my psychiatrist—Dr. Rosenberg says that if anyone should be blamed, it should be you. That you brought it all upon yourself, everything—even the accident. *(Pause.)* How could that be, you say? Well, I'll tell you. Dr. Rosenberg—she's a lady, by the way—Sarah Rosenberg—sometimes I wonder if I ever could have been a doctor. I'd never have been able to get through medical school—cutting up all those little animals and things—would have turned my stomach—anyway, Dr. Rosenberg says it's not my fault and I shouldn't hate myself for it. I need to reconcile with the past, she said, so that's why I came to visit you on your birthday. *(Pause.)* Ten years of therapy with Dr. Rosenberg—they made me go every week—suicidal, they said I was. *(Pause.)* She said it all started when daddy walked out on us. I was only twelve years old then, Grace, but you tried to blame that on me. I loved my daddy and I know he loved me. The problem was, he hated you. You never let up on him. Pecking at him all the time. Never saw you hug or kiss him or even happy to see him come home. I don't blame him for running off with Sue-Ellen Makepeace. By the by, daddy came to visit me regular while I was away. Told me a lot about the relationship between you and him. How you cried for days when you got pregnant. I always knew you never wanted me. You made that clear to me on a number of occasions. Now, here I am, on your birthday, standing on your grave. *(She toasts Grace.)* That's when you started drinking a lot, after daddy left. Soon you were drunk every night, filling my head with so much negativity about daddy, and men in general, that by the time I was eighteen I was a lush, just like you. Cheap bourbon and cheap champagne—what a way to grow up. Boys never wanted to take me out, because I smelled of whiskey and tobacco. You turned me into a cripple, like yourself—ruining my life like yours had been ruined—chasing off any chance of me finding love or happiness. *(Pause.)* Dr. Rosenberg said you were a very bitter and unhappy woman—that you felt there was no fulfillment in your life and because of it you didn't want me to be happy. That's what happened the night of the accident. *(Pause.)* Peter Presley was the only boy who ever took a real liking to me. He was a very sensitive young man. I was so thrilled when he asked me to accompany him to the country pie bake-off. I felt so special, as though he probably saw through the liquor—through the pain—saw the beautiful person I was inside and wanted to bring it out. *(Angry.)* How could you have done that to me, Grace. That was so cruel. I was so upset when he didn't come to call—so disappointed and hurt. It was just chance that made me run into him in town a few days later. How do you think I felt when he told me he was sorry I was under the weather when he came to call on me at the house. I felt so humiliated and embarrassed—so angry—that moment I hated you so much I wished you were dead—I never wanted to see you again. *(She composes herself.)* Dr. Rosenberg said it was the liquor. You were so drunk when I got home, you didn't even remember Peter coming by that day. It didn't even matter to you that you shattered my life. *(Pause.)* I tried to punish you the only way I knew how, by taking your liquor from you. Did you think I was bringing it up to my room so I could have it all to myself? *(Pause.)* Dr. Rosenberg said if you never came up the stairs after me, it never would have happened. *(Pause.)* You shouldn't have grabbed me, Grace. You shouldn't have hit me. Do you remember how you hit me? You wouldn't stop—it was the liquor—that's what Dr. Rosenberg said—you were drunk—all I wanted to do was push you away—to stop you from hitting me—Dr. Rosenberg said drunks can't keep their balance—that's why you went over the railing. *(Pause.)* I've relived that moment in slow motion every day for the last ten years. Ten years locked up for something I didn't mean to do, that you brought upon yourself. *(Pause.)* Do I miss you? Some. I'll get over it. Am I sorry? I've never come to terms with that. I'm closer to daddy now. He says we are going to make up for all the time that has been lost now that I'm out and he doesn't have to contend with you. Sue-Ellen makes him real happy. Most importantly, however, is that I am sober and that I have learned to control my drinking instead of it controlling me. I don't have to drink this whole bottle anymore but I betcha you'd sure like a drink now, wouldn't you Grace. You never could pass up the chance to have another drink. Even when you had the D.T.'s, you'd want more just to get "straight", you called it. Well, allow me to do the honors. *(She pours the rest of the champagne onto her grave.)* Go ahead—drink up, Grace—and happy birthday. *(Blackout.)*

Hot Air

Richard Willett

Scene: here and now

Serio-Comic
June: a woman remembering her past, 30s

*Here, restless, June compares her current lover to her first
lover.*

JUNE: I was groomed to be a debutante, but I used my looks to
become queen of the smoke hole. I could have had my pick of
the football team, but I went after Lance Luder. His teammates
were well-groomed boys from good families, with squeaky clean
bodies my parents would have been proud to see me join at the
altar. Lance had jet-black hair and dark eyes and a beard that
made him look like Lucifer. When us bad girls discussed it in the
john, there was never any argument: Lance Luder had to have the
biggest, meanest, hairiest dick in our whole high school. I don't
know what he was doing on the football team, except maybe trying to please his dad. Those rough boys would always get silly
sentimental over their dads, I found. I could make them grunt
and heave and say "oh, baby" a couple million times, but when
they'd start talking about their dads, you'd think: Now there's a
boy I could really fall for. Angel with a Hades passport. The other
night I said to Danny…one of those things I'm always saying
these days, something like "We're just not connecting anymore,"
and he got all bright-eyed and bushy tailed and went into his
problem-solver mode, telling me he sensed that, too, and that we
should "work" on it. Lance Luder never discussed a feeling with
me once. But when we'd trudge through the woods behind our
school with Debbie Troy and Billy Talbot, on the way to our secret
spot, he and Billy would do their broken-down renditions of rock
lyrics and claim they spoke from the heart. I can still smell the

beer on his sweet breath, the squeak of his leather jacket sleeves as he hovered over me, all boyish now in memory, but nothing but a man at the time. Football pecs in a Handsworth Secondary T-shirt, and when we were done his boots had dug canals in the dirt. Danny talks as if I've saved his life. There's a breathless quality to his enthusiasm, but a joyful breathlessness, as if he yearns for a kind of death. The smothering, for him, you see, somehow sustains life. The last time I was home, I went through the phone book, looking up names of people I'd known, seeing if they were still there. But I never called one of them. I found myself preoccupied instead by a photo in the local paper of the current football team from my old high school. There's one of them every year, it seems. In the circle of crewcutted, bright-eyed young athletes, one boy smirked more than smiled, with a black goatee and a big ring in his ear and eyes that said, "I will totally fuck you up." And I don't want to discuss my feelings. And I don't want to be reasonable. And I don't want to be happy. I want to be young and stupid.

Infrared

Mac Wellman in collaboration with Jane Geiser

Scene: NYC and the Infrared mirror world

Dramatic
Cathy X: a young woman with a shocking dual identity, 20s

> *A quirk of dimensional displacement has landed Cathy X in the mirror image world of Infrared where she determines to act as a missionary of the soul. Here, she preaches to Infrared's inhabitants.*

CATHY X: People and animals do certain things because they believe they have come across a hole, because they want to dig a hole, to pass through a hole, to jump over a hole, or to hide inside one. *(Pause.)* Holes, like shadows and persons, are spacio-temporally localized beings. And like these too, they may best be thought of as temporary disturbances. *(Pause.)* Holes, like shadows, have hosts and like shadows are dependent upon these for existence. *(Pause.)* Holes and shadows, like the lilies of the field toil not; they accompany us in our labors and in our pleasures; they remind us of the insubstantiality of our vainglorious wishful thinking. *(Pause.)* And so I came out of a world on the Other Side in order to redeem you all, the lost ones from the folly of your ways; for it is the folly and wretchedness of the inhabitants of Infrared that you are always mistaking wrong for right; just as you mistake holes for shadows and shadows for holes. *(Pause.)* And it is my task to set the matter right and show you the way to redemption is paved with the stones of mercy and forgiveness, stones which sparkle like the scales of the dragon...

James Bond's Old Girlfriends

Toni Schlesinger

Scene: here and now

Serio-Comic
Linda: a former Bond Girl, 40–60

> *Here, a onetime starlet recounts the chance meeting of a former comrade in arms at a Del-Mart.*

LINDA: Was I surprised! I was in the Del-Mart,deciding on a pair of eyebrow tweezers when I looked over at the woman working the cash register and I realized she was the one from—Budapest! I knew her thirty years ago when we were both making a film with James—James Bond—dah dah…dah! Like me, she had been one of James Bond's Old Girl Friends. The night I met her she was eating chicken paprikash at a restaurant overlooking the Danube— on the West side. I was having the goulash. She was wearing a pale green sheath with shoes died to match. Her sunglasses were from Rome. Starting from the top of her head was a long ponytail. We called her Pony in keeping with her hairstyle. She wore a head scarf. We *all* wore head scarves. That's because our hair would get messed up when we had to ride in the hydrofoils and speed boats…with James—James Bond. Pony was James Bond's favorite. I enjoyed the way she did the Monkey. I did the Monkey, too. I had Courreges boots. But Pony did it better. And she got to be in the scene where the girls give James a sponge bath near the volcano. She was the one brushing the dog in the fan tan parlor who rushes out the door…tears off her evening gown…under which she is wearing a frogman suit.

She dives in the sea…has a fight with two other frogmen and wins…and later has toast on the yacht…for my scene, I had to stand on the back of a sea turtle and adjust the strap of my diving mask…Well thirty years later here's Pony at the Del-Mart, wearing a smock and working the cash register. I could barely contain myself. I ran over. "Pony, Pony," I said. "Linda, Linda," she said. "Your hair." "My hair. Where's your ponytail." "It went away, " she said. "That's too bad." "It happens." Then Pony filled me in. Tishy, who had been another one of the girlfriends—she's living in Switzerland, she married a Dutch man, they got three kids, one cuter than the next. Tishy didn't last long as a girlfriend. She got seasick all the time and couldn't ride on the yachts the way the rest of us could. Mr. Broccoli, the producer, said Tishy had been chosen for her vulnerability. I was chosen for my serenity and maturity. They wanted Pony for her mysteriousness. While Pony checked through a man with a lawn chair—we reminisced. "Remember the publicity shots," she said—"the one with you, me, James Bond, the production designer, and Mr. Broccoli." "Yes," I said, "and the one where you got to stand next to James Bond with your ponytail flipped out over your shoulders Grecian style." "Go on, I was just one of the girls...wait, I gotta get some quarters." She came back, cracked open a roll on the side of the drawer, bagged some mothballs for a woman wearing a rain bonnet... I asked her—how'd you come to work at the Del-Mart." "It's a long story," she said, "but after I stopped being one of the girlfriends, I came back to the States and worked the Spokane Environmental Fair. I married a panicky carnival barker who killed himself. Then I came east to Brooklyn. I got a place in Williamsburg, a two flat, with beige concrete moulding. I got a hide-a-bed, a mahogany dining set, and an oscillating fan. You should come for dinner sometime. *(Linda back in the present.)* *Right!* I'm going to go to Brooklyn. Hah. You know I used to want to be Pony so badly—not anymore. Her upper arms are flabby. Mine aren't so great. I should be grateful I have two but still. Her legs used to be so long—she couldn't cross them underneath a counter. Now they're short. It's amazing. I hate her lipstick color. And that Del-Mart—the prices are never marked on the items. They always have to call for a price check. How can she work there. As for me...I do some voice-over work. I have an apartment on Park Avenue...at the Stanley. I have a Fendi handbag and—I am still...very...pretty. *(Blackout.)*

The Lady With The Toy Dog

Sari Bodi

Adapted from *The Lady With the Toy Dog* by Anton Chekhov

Scene: a resort on Yalta, the turn of the century

Dramatic
Anna: a young woman who has been unfaithful to her husband, 20s

> *While on holiday in Yalta, Anna has become involved with the unscrupulous Dimitri. Here, she indulges in a bit of self-loathing.*

ANNA: How can I justify myself? No, I am a wicked, fallen woman! I despise myself, and have no desire to justify myself! It isn't my husband I have deceived, but myself! I have been deceiving myself for a long time. My husband may be a good, honest man, but he is a flunky. When I married him I was twenty. I was devoured with curiosity. I longed for something better. Surely, I told myself, there is another kind of life. I wanted to live. To live, only to live!

[DIMITRI: I don't understand. What do you want?]

ANNA: You do not understand it, but I swear by God I could no longer control myself. Something strange was going on in me. I could not hold back. I told my husband I was ill, and I came to Yalta…And here I have been walking about dizzily, like a lunatic. Now I am nothing but a low, common woman whom anyone may despise.

[DIMITRI: Don't, don't. It's like you're playing a part in a melodrama.]

ANNA: Believe me, I beg you. I love all that is honest and pure in life, and sin is revolting to me. I don't know what I am doing. There are simple people who say, "The devil entrapped me," and now I can say of myself that the Evil One has led me astray.

The Lady With The Toy Dog

Sari Bodi

Adapted from *The Lady With the Toy Dog* by Anton Chekhov

Scene: a resort on Yalta, the turn of the century

Dramatic
Anna: a young woman who has been unfaithful to her husband, 20s

> *Anna has tasted both passion and freedom during her holiday in Yalta. When her forgotten husband sends a telegram demanding that she return home, Anna wonders if she will able to go back to her old life.*

ANNA: *(Holds a telegram and talks to her dog.)* Telegrams are never good news, my little Pomeranian. No one will ever send you a telegram to say, "You will soon experience happiness." No, a telegram is a reminder that life is hard. That before you received the telegram, the sky was blue and the sea lilac colored, but now, life will be brown again. I can hear my husband's words in this telegram even though I have not yet read it. Here, can you hear them? Cold, hard words from Petersburg. "Come home. I need you." You know my husband never wastes words. I cannot even remember him asking me to marry him, it was so to the point. You were there with me, chewing a bone, I recall. You should have stopped me from saying "yes." It is right he should work in the government, where he can smoke cigars and speak foolishly with the other government employees. He controls everything I do. It's as if he knew I experienced some joy for the first time last night. I look different today, don't I? He thinks that we are the same person, that marriage joins two people together so that their thoughts merge. He will say, "I like roasted cabbage, and Anna does as well." or "I think that opera is a silly bother, and so does Anna." I adore opera. When I listen to the heroine sing, I can see that someone else has as horrible a life as I. And now I have to go home to this life. To pretend that I like roasted cabbage, and hate opera, and love my husband. When all the time, I will be wishing that my fate was different. That I had met Dimitri Dimitrich before I married my husband, and before he met his wife. And then I would never have received this telegram. I could throw it into the sea. But it would not matter. It would keep returning to me like a letter in a bottle.

Lesbian's Last Pizza

Jeff Goode

Scene: here and now

Serio-Comic
A Lesbian: a woman preparing to commit suicide, 30–40

> *Here, a woman dying of AIDS phones her mother to say good-bye before taking her own life via drug overdose.*

LESBIAN: *(She holds the phone for a long time, smiling. Mischievously.)* Two can play at this game…Mom, if you'll talk to me I'll give ya a dollar…All right, let me sweeten the pot. If you talk to me, I'll give you… *(She looks in her pocket.)* Two dollars…Come on, two dollars, Mom, it's all I've got. *(No response.)* You know who I saw yesterday? Michael. He forgives me, Mom. He even brought me flowers. They were beautiful. Golden roses. Like the kind we had at our wedding. Well, we didn't have them. They were already there. In the garden outside the chapel. They were so beautiful I had to throw them away. They reminded me too much…So maybe he doesn't forgive me. Maybe he came to punish me. With flowers. Well, I threw them away, so I guess I won that round…Some things can never be forgiven…You don't forgive me, do you, Mom? For divorcing Michael. For not giving you grandchildren. For *marrying* Michael. For dropping out of college. For growing up. And having a personality that wasn't the same as yours. Or for having a personality too much like yours. For stealing the little girl away from you who looked so cute in her pastel jumper and the skinned knee and the half a broken popsicle crying in that picture you showed everyone at Thanksgiving every year, until you found out about Linda. For being born. No, that's not fair. You don't have to say anything, I take it back. You forgave me for being born. I never forgave you. Mom, if I forgive you for that, will you come see me?…I'll have to think about it. Some things are unforgivable. Oh! um, Mom, I got a call on the other line. Hold on, okay?...Okay? Mom?... Whatever. *(She changes lines.)* Hello?

Lesbian's Last Pizza

Jeff Goode

Scene: here and now

Serio-Comic
A Lesbian: a woman preparing to commit suicide, 30–40

> *Here, the dying lesbian calls her father, to whom she hasn't spoken in years, to say good-bye.*

LESBIAN: "Dad." Hi…Guess who this is. *(Her eyes widen. She leaps out of her chair.)* AGH!! You sick fuck! This is your daughter! Yes, it's your daughter, you disgusting pig! You're scum, do you know that, Dad? Damn right you're sorry! You're a sorry excuse. Is that how you'd talk to anyone? Ugh! I'd never speak to you again, if I didn't think this was going to be the worst conversation of your life. You pig! You disgusting sick fuck pig…Yeah, I missed you, too. Yeah right. Then why didn't you come to my wedding? Yeah, I got married. Surprise. Thanks, I guess. I *sent* you an invitation…I sent you an invitation! Mom sent it. Why would she do that? I don't believe you. Well, you should have…found out or something…Well thanks, I guess. Nobody you know. No, no kids. Well, for one thing I saw how yours turned out. You'd like that, though, wouldn't you? A couple of adorable grandkids to convince yourself that something good came out of you and Mom. Well, I got news for ya, Pop. I'm divorced. Yeah, that's a whole chapter of my life you missed out on. I guess you'll never know. Actually, I'll send you a photo. I'll send you a whole press packet. Pictures, anecdotes. Everything you need to know to bring you up to date on everything about my life that doesn't matter anymore because it's over and you missed it. Yeah, you're pathetic, Dad. I didn't call for an apology. Why do you think I called?…*You have no idea.* You can't possibly know. Do you realize that, Dad? You don't know me! Do you remember the time you had to drive me to school for the band concert. And we got that flat. And I was standing there crying while you tried to change the tire in the rain. And we finally got there but the concert had already started, and you dropped me off backstage but I was too embarrassed to go out on stage so I hid in the wings. And played my little flute behind the curtains. You remember that, don't you, Dad? Because afterwards you told me I played beautifully. I'm not that person anymore, Dad. I'm not that little girl. I turned thirty. I'm married and divorced. Today if I arrived late for that concert, I'd march right out on that stage anyway and take my seat in the flute section. And I'd pull out my harmonica and join in on the next song. And I wouldn't have been late anyway because I'd've changed the flat for you, 'cause I *hate* standing in the rain. And that's who I am. And you don't know that because you didn't care enough to find out. *(Taken aback.)* You're what? You got married? When? Why didn't you tell me? I would've come. You should have called me yourself. Because you didn't call me. I'd have called you if you had called me! You didn't call me first. Well, who…when did it happen? Of course I wanted to be there…You didn't call me. I would have called you if you had called me. You're what? You're divorced?…Touché…um, listen, Dad, I know this is going to sound rude. But I don't want to talk about anything you want to talk about. *(Pause, not sure where to begin.)* You would have liked him, Dad. Michael my husband. Ex. Husband. He liked to fish…I don't know why I married Michael. But it wasn't for love. I know that now, because…That's why I divorced him. Because I fell in love. With someone else. With…with…With someone else…And…she…died. Yes. That's exactly what I am. Still miss me? Dad, I'm afraid we're pressed for time, so you're gonna have to skip denial and anger and go right to acceptance. Because there's more. Are you sitting down? I called—ha ha ha—you know, I feel better already, Dad. Oh my God. You know, I think I'm going to feel great when I tell you this. Ha ha. I think this is going to make my day. Dad, Linda…died of…AIDS. Ha ha. I'm dying…of AIDS…oh fuck…oh fuck. So I guess I just called to say "Hi." And "bye." And fuck you and I love you, and… *(She slams the phone down, three times. She looks at the phone.)* And why did you get married?…The first time. No, the second time. No, the first time.

Losers Of The Big Picture

Robert Vivian

Scene: a summer house

Dramatic
Elizabeth: a woman on the verge of momentous change, 50s

> *Elizabeth has come to realize the emptiness in her life as a signal for change. She has therefore resolved to leave her husband for a new life as a volunteer worker in Africa. When her family pressures her to stay, she makes the following declaration.*

ELIZABETH: You want me to surrender. You want me to succumb. Then everything will be in order again and you can resume your destructive ways. Suddenly you feel threatened. Suddenly I'm significant because I challenge the eternal order of things. I'm the wife who's moving out and forsaking her domestic duties. Blow jobs in the closet and endless trips to the grocery store for all the cravings of your craven little heart. But I had a brain once. And a heart. And wild, improbable dreams. I had to give them up halfway through because my partner reneged on his part of the deal. I could remain the same. Learn to live with the hypocrisy and the plastic hangers. My kind has been threatened with extinction before. But then I saw a ship coming on the horizon, coming toward me in a terrible dream. I tried to block it out but it blocked out the rest of my life. I had no choice. I kept telling myself, This isn't the time for a revolution, but the ship kept coming. Bigger. Larger. Faster than before. More imposing in line and structure. I am not the woman you think I am. I am not the woman. I have lived too long, scheming and planning for the day that will never come. I want my ship of woe. I want it. And if you try to keep me from going, I'll scratch your eyes out. I have to leave. I have to sail away. I have no meaning in my life. Don't you understand?

Losers Of The Big Picture

Robert Vivian

Scene: a summer house

Dramatic
Jean: an aging alcoholic, 50s

> *When her sister-in-law accuses her of having killed her husband, Fritz, by enabling his drinking, Jean readily agrees.*

JEAN: *(Tilts mask back on her forehead.)* Yes. I killed him. It's my turn to tremble, to shake like one of your goddamned leaves. I killed him. Drank him to death like you said. Said, Here, Fritz, have a drink of this: Here, Fritz, I don't love you anymore: Here, Fritz, you're a failure: Here, Fritz, why don't you win the Nobel Prize: Here, Fritz, what are you afraid of: Here, Fritz, I didn't mean it: Here, Fritz, I'm gonna kill myself: Here, Fritz, I don't believe in God: Here, Fritz, I married a weakling: Here, Fritz, why do you make those stupid, pathetic lightbulbs: Here, Fritz, I adore your little lights, your little X-mas trees, your little choo-choos. *Here, Fritz. (Pause.)* Good enough for you? What I did to him? Tore a man right down in front of your eyes when he had more sense, more compassion, more genius than any other man I've ever known? I don't know what got into me. Okay? It's implausible. Impossible. Out of whack and in character and I hate myself for it, my ability to tear down. I'm a human wrecking ball. But make no mistake: the ball will make a loop-de-loop and knock my scattered brains out. And then Fritz will have to forgive me, even if I have chase him down the portals of God's blue heaven.

Many Colors Make The Thunder-King

Femi Osofisan

Scene: the kingdom of King Shango

Dramatic
Oya: the king's first wife, 20–30

> *When Shango finds true love with his second wife, Osun, Oya's jealousy drives her to commit desperate acts of betrayal. Here, the jealous queen vents her rage.*

OYA: He's always with her, but not with me. He has abundant time for her caprices, But when I demand attention, he has a thousand excuses! I've seen the secret looks they exchange, The unspoken messages which pass between them. I've seen the way they touch each other, even across a room, with messages of tenderness! He used to be mine, all mine. All these looks were mine! All these tender touches were mine, mine! And now he's going to take a third wife! Oh you gods, you know! When she comes, Oya will no longer exist! I'll have to go back to my old loneliness in the depths of the river! I know my womb is fertile! I know it, I see the proof every month! But it is he who won't come to me when I'm ready for him! Children are not mere wastrels after all! They just don't come into the world like that. They have to know that they are wanted by their future parents. That they're coming to a house of love. So it's his fault that my children have remained in heaven and refused to come down! He treats me like a discarded rag, but I will prove to him I am Oya! I am no longer going to wait for him! If he will not cultivate his field, then I will find someone else to do it for him!

Migrant Voices

Martha King DeSilva

Scene: a backyard, and a homestead in the Texas panhandle

Serio-comic
Sarah: a young girl with a vivid imagination, 8–11

Here, young Sarah describes in detail her favorite pastime: pretending.

SARAH: *(A young girl is standing against a fence. Her mother is in the distance watching her.)* Mama doesn't like me to go far. She tells me to play inside the fence so she can keep her eye on me while she works. I do what she tells me. 'Cause I'm good. I play all day by myself until it gets dark. I play pretend. I have a pretend family. I'm the mommy. I'm really pretty and I wear dresses all the time and shoes with bows on them. And lipstick. I've got rings on all my fingers. And I smell good. There's a daddy too. He's handsome and rich. His name is Robert, though sometimes it's Thomas. He drives a car. I don't know what kind. But it's big. And it's got a seat in the back on the outside. The pretend house we live in is purple. That's my favorite color. And it's got lots and lots of flowers in the front. And a tree for climbing. I don't climb the tree though, 'cause I'm the mommy. I'm a really good mommy. I've got three babies. They're fat and have curly hair. All of 'em. They never, ever cry though. They sleep and they laugh a lot. We have a kitchen in our house, too. I need a kitchen 'cause I have to cook for our family. For dinner last night we had chicken and potatoes with butter. No vegetables. *(She makes a face.)* And I made the biggest, hugest chocolate cake. It was really good and I had three pieces. Oh and we had ice cream. We always have ice cream. Chocolate or strawberry. Sometimes we go out for a drive in the car. And sometimes I drive! I'm a good driver. *(She makes driving noises.)* Vroom, vroom…Oh, and we also have a radio. It's

51

in our parlor. It cost a lot of money to get but it's the best kind. It's this big and it plays music. I don't let the babies touch the radio 'cause they might break it. Mama doesn't like when I play pretend. I have to do it kinda quiet. She got mad at me the last time when she heard me talkin to the babies. I'm too old for that, she said. She said that there aren't any babies, and that I don't have a car, and that there isn't a daddy, either. She made me come sit by her really close while she was doing the wash so she could make sure I wasn't pretending. She told me to go inside and get my Annie and play with that. Annie's this doll I have. The only one. She's not pretty at all. When I got her, she was kind of dirty and her hair was half out of her head. Mama fixed her up a little and put a hat on her head to make her nice but I still don't like her. Sometimes when I'm not playing pretend, I draw. I take my favorite stick and I draw in the dirt. It's not as fun as pretending but it's pretty good. I'm a good drawer. I draw birds and suns and flowers and people. All my people have smiles on them. Mama wants me to work on my letters. She says I should write my name. S.A.R.A.H. I have trouble with my S's. Sometimes I do them backwards. I don't go to school but Mama wants me to learn stuff anyway. Like reading. And numbers. I don't like to. I like pretending most. Mama and Daddy talk about me when they think I'm not listening. Mostly at night. After I go to bed. They say that I'm bad because I talk to myself all the time and that I see things that aren't there. Mama thinks maybe I would stop if I had some chores to do. They say maybe I pretend because I'm too dumb to do anything else. I have a new pretend. I'm captured by bad people and put in a jail. I pretend this fence is my jail. It's a good jail, isn't it? I'm all by myself and it's cold and dark. I only eat once a day. And there's no one to talk to except the guards who are pretty mean. The guards want to get me to talk. To tell them the secrets I know. But I don't do this. I don't say anything. It's all inside me. They think they can make me feel bad, but they can't. 'Cause I'm strong. When I start my pretend, I'm in the jail for a hundred billion years. Nobody believes it. I always get out at the end. In different ways each time. Sometimes I sneak over the fence. Other times, I close my eyes and say magic, secret words and I'm in a new place. Other times, I trick the guards and escape when they think I'm asleep. I can make my pretend really bad if I want. I can make it so the guards hurt me. The other day, I scratched myself with the fence. I tore my dress and now I have a sore. See? It didn't hurt at all. And I got out. Mama got scared when she saw it. I didn't tell her about the guards. It's one of the best pretends I think I've ever had. It's best because it always starts out bad. But it always ends up good. 'Cause I escape.

Migrant Voices
Martha King DeSilva

Scene: a backyard, and a homestead in the Texas panhandle

Dramatic
A grieving mother, 30s

> *Here, a careworn farmer's wife remembers her daughter's death.*

MOTHER: I'm not much good at talkin. And I don't ever talk about myself, really. What's there to say? I don't know… *(She thinks.)* I'm a wife. A mother. *(Definitively.)* A farmer. Max is my husband and we have two children—Emma and Andrew. *(A pause.)* We used to have three. Liza died when she was just a baby. She was, oh, just three months old, I guess. *(She remembers.)* That was back in, uh, February of '38. Right after we came to the Panhandle. Durin' the worst winter I can remember. Terrible cold and dust storms. We was livin in a one room shack. *(She is picturing it.)* Dirt floor. Two cots along one wall. A stove in the corner. One night, in the middle of winter, a blue norther comes in. It was freezin in the shack, and we kep fillin the stove with anything we could find to burn. Liza been cryin all night with a fever. Cryin and cryin. *(She covers her ears at the memory.)* Her mouth had gotten so swolled up, she couldn't even take my milk. And all I could think was, "Please God Almighty make her stop." I rocked her and sang to her and tried to bring down the fever with a wet cloth. Early in the morning, she seemed to settle and sleep. So I lay her down on Max and my bed… *(She is remembering a moment.)* I fergit how I knew, but I touched her cheek and it was cold and there was no breath coming from her neither. Her tiny body was all clenched-up like. And she was gone. *(She acknowledges but this is hard for her.)* It was a relief to me. God had stopped her cryin like I asked. We buried her in the frozen

54

backyard, just as the sun was comin up. Didn't have a box to put her in or nothing, just a torn blanket. It took Max forever to dig far enough down, I remember. The ground was so hard. He put the last shovelful of dirt on her grave. "That's it," I said. *(She just realizes.)* I don't think I even looked back. Anyways, we walked back inside. Then I made a porridge for the children. Max sat down in a chair and put his head in his hands and cried. I just looked at him. One less mouth to feed, I thought. That night I couldn't sleep and I lay in bed a long time. *(She remembers.)* You know, Liza used to sleep between Max and me...I remember I used to like to listen to her little breathin. Max was asleep aside me. I got up and went to the door. We keep a rifle above it. Protection. I stood on a box and pulled it down. I put a torn coat over my shoulders and went out back. I don't remember if it was cold or not. Must've been, though, hmmm? But I remember the moon. Big and full. The ground was flat except for the little mound where Liza was. I looked at it. I sat down on a crate and thought for a long time...oh, I don't know. 'Bout everythin. The rifle was gettin cold in my hands and it felt heavy. Kinda power-ful. Smooth, sort of. I pushed my hair back from my face and leaned over and opened my mouth. Do you know, I could taste the metal with my tongue? My finger reached for the trigger. I closed my eyes. *(Pause.)* And I felt...I don't know what you'd call it. Comfort maybe? *(Decides.)* Peace. My shoulders dropped and it was like I could feel the ache go out of 'em. I don't know how long I sat out there like that. Just twistin the gun back and forth in my hands. Back and forth. The moon was high in the sky when Max came out. He saw me, gun in my mouth and sat close aside me without a word. I listened to the wind. To the sound of breathin in Max's chest. I could smell his jacket—a musty smell that I loved. I look at his hands propped on his knees, curved a lit-tle. I pulled the gun from my mouth and set it beside me. Then I leaned over and threw up. And I cried. Cried so loud and long, I could hear it in the night air. Max took me in his arms then. He kissed my hair. *(She motions toward her hairline.)* That made me cry more. After a while, we went back into the house, Max with his arm around me. *(Realizes.)* I haven't thought of that night in a long while. I don't like to. It hurts me. *(She tries to articulate it.)* Hurts me how…I could lose my beautiful baby girl and not feel sad. And how I wished for it, almos. Max never asks me about it neither. Never. The rifle is gone. I don know what happened to it. Just as well. I don't really understand any of this. All I know is if you die, you're dead, that's all. And I guess there isn't anything more than that.

The Mineola Twins

Paula Vogel

Scene: America during the Eisenhower Administration

Serio-Comic
Myra: the bad twin, 17

Here, devilish Myra remembers a surrealistic air raid drill.

MYRA: So. It was like homeroom, only we were calculating the hypotenuse of hygiene. I whispered to Billy Bonnell—what does that mean? And he said: Yuck-yuck—it's the same angle as the triangle under your skirt, Myra Richards. Yuck-yuck. Shut-Up Creep! Thhwwack! My metal straightedge took off the top of his cranium. And then Mrs. Hopkins said, in this voice from the crypt: Miss Richards—what is the hypotenuse of the square root of hygiene? And just as I was saying Excuse Me, Mrs. Hopkins, But I Didn't Know What the Homework Was for Today on Account of Being Suspended Last Week By You 'Cause of the Dumb-Ass Dress Code—The Voice Cuts In on the Intercom: *"...Get...To... the...Door...Now."* And we all got real scared. And the Nuclear Air Raid Siren Came On, Real Loud. And kids started bawling and scrambling under their desks. Somehow we knew it was For Real. We could hear this weird harmony of the bombs whistling through space. And we could see the bombs in slow motion coming for us, with a straight line drawn from Moscow to Mineola. Dead Center for the Nassau County Courthouse. Dead Center for Roosevelt Field. And Dead Center for Mineola High. Home of the Mineola Mustangs. And I knew it would do diddly-squat to get under the desk. I looked at the clock, frozen at five minutes to twelve. And Something drew me into the hall, out of the maw of that classroom. Into the hall, where there was pulsing red light and green smoke. Like Christmas in Hell. Kids' bodies were mangled everywhere. Our principal Mr. Chotliner was hypotenusing under Miss Dorothy Comby's skirt, in the middle of the hall. And the kids in Detention Hall were watching. I just kept walking. Lockers were opening and shutting like gills in a deepwater fish, singing "Peggy Sue" each time they opened. I just kept walking. The girls' Glee Club had spread-eagled Mr. Koch the driver's ed. instructor further down the hall, and they were getting the long-handled custodian's broom out of the closet. I just kept walking. I checked my watch. Five minutes to the Apocalypse. I could hear the bombs humming louder now. I thought of crossing against the lights and getting home. But There's nothing lonelier than watching your parents hug while you curl up on the rug alone and Mom's ceramic dogs melt on the mantle as the sky glows its final Big Red. Then I heard The Voice on the intercom say to me: *"Find...Her..."* I had to Obey The Voice. I knew that at the bottom of the stairwell, I would find my twin sister Myrna, hiding from me. Curled up in a little O, her back to me. Just like Old Times in the womb. A Little O trying to float away from me.

[The Voice begins to breathe rapidly into the microphone.]

MYRA: I entered the stairwell at the top. The lights were out. There was a thickness to the air. The stairs were steep. And I heard her soft breathing, trying not to breathe. She could hear me breathe. Her soft neck, trying not to swallow.

[The amplified sound of The Voice gulping.]

MYRA: She could taste my saliva. Her heart, trying not to beat.

[The amplified sound of a beating heart.]

MYRA: She could hear my heart thunder.

[The heart beats faster.]

MYRA: She knew I was there. And I said: *"I'm Coming, Myrna. I'm Coming...to Find...You..."*

The Mineola Twins

Paula Vogel

Scene: America during the Eisenhower Administration

Serio-Comic
Myra: the bad twin, 17

> *After sleeping with her twin sister's fiancé, Myra tries to con-*
> *vince the straight-laced young man to go out on the town*
> *with her.*

> *(There is a heap in the bed beside her, curled under the cheap*
> *chintz spread, completely covered, and hogging the entire*
> *bedspread. Occasionally, we hear muffled sobs.)*

MYRA: "I Like Ike. I Like Ike." I mean, is that cornball or what? Can you believe how way-in this country is? They like some bald, golfing dude whose idea of a hot time is having Mamie stroke his clubs! They voted for that square twice! "I Like Ike—" I mean, that is yo-yo's-ville. *(She stops, pops her gum. Listens to the heap.)* Hey, man. Hey, daddy. I'm trying to see? I'm trying to "engage," dig? I'm dishing politics, man, I'm trying to connect. *(She nudges the heap.)* Hey. Hey. You gonna come out sometime this decade? *(The heap covers itself with some insistence.)* Hey. Suit yourself, daddy-o. No skin offa my pearly whites. I've had cats cry before the Act, and I've had lotsa cats wail during. You're the first one to boo-hoo after. *(She waits for a response. Tries again.)* Hey, I gotta idea. You got any bread? Any wheels? We could just spook in your bomb and get some burgers. Or We go peel on outta here and spin into the Village. It's crazy down there, any night of the week. We go take in the Vanguard—do you dig that scene? It's the most, the meanest...we could do a set, and then blow the joint and just walk around the streets. There's this one guy, Ace, who walks around with a *parrot* on his shoulder. It's crazy. He's so hip—you pay him a dime, and he gives you a poem, on the spot. He poetizes on a dime. And these poems— they don't rhyme or anything. They're deep. They don't *mean,* they just *are.* It's far-out!

Miracles

Frank Higgins

Scene: a private school for autistic children

Dramatic
Kate: a teacher of autistic children, 30–40

> *Kate claims to have made an amazing breakthrough in com-*
> *munication with one of her students, a young woman*
> *named Eve who has written a book while "speaking" to Kate*
> *via computer keyboard. Here, Kate expresses a rather nega-*
> *tive worldview to Eve's concerned father.*

KATE: Well…I don't know if I want to be out in that world too much.

[TOM: That world?]

KATE: In that world people call it a miracle if they can make a bra that makes your boobs bigger. So I work here.

[TOM: Copout.]

KATE: Really, there's no mystery to me…Okay. Have you ever looked at much modern art?

[TOM: Some.]

KATE: Ever looked at cancer cells under a microscope?

[TOM: Yes.]

KATE: They look just like a lot of modern art. I went to a gallery opening and the walls were *filled* with this stuff; everybody oohs and ahs, but to me it looks like the walls are all filled with cancer. That's what I think of the times we're living in. We're surrounded by things that are cancer for our soul, but most of us look at the things killing us and think 'how nice.'

[TOM: You're passionate about this.]

KATE: Well it's important. Here we are sticking our toe into outer space, ready to take the big plunge—if the meek *do* inherit the earth, it'll be because the bold left for a better planet—and we're exploring the bottoms of the seas, we're just about at the point science will be able to *clone* somebody. You'd think we were living in the greatest of times, but we're living in a dead culture with dead ideals, and all our busy *activity* is just the flapping around of a fish thrown on the dock.

Miracles

Frank Higgins

Scene: a private school for autistic children

Dramatic
Kate: a teacher of autistic children, 30–40

> *Kate claims to be able to communicate with seventeen-year-old Eve by "facilitating" the autistic girl's use of a keyboard. When Eve's father begins to suspect that Kate has fabricated everything that Eve has supposedly said via the keyboard, he storms out of the school with threats to remove Eve. Here, Kate desperately pleads with an unresponsive Eve to communicate.*

KATE: We can't have you with tears on your cheeks. You know what I used to do when I was little and somebody made me cry? I'd get a tiny little spoon, like a spoon you pick up olives with? And I'd put the spoon under the corners of my eyes and I'd collect my tears in that spoon. And then I'd fling the tears at whoever made me cry; I'd show *them.* If you wanted to fling tears at me right now, I wouldn't blame you. I'm sorry we got loud and made you upset. This is your home; you shouldn't have to put up with that. Let me have your wrist. *(Kate takes Eve's wrist.)* Eve, I need you to say something now. Say anything you want but say *something. (No typing.)* Eve, don't be this way. It's important. You have to talk to me like you did before. *(No typing.)* I'm sorry we were shouting; I'm sorry. Let's whisper. Can you type just a vowel for me? *(No typing.)* Eve, we can't start all over from scratch. Remember how hard that was? How long before we got anything done?…Eve, I'm not going to quit on you. I'm not a quitter. But I need you to help me right now, okay? Maybe we'll wind up staying here all night coz I am not leaving until you talk to me again. *(No typing.)* Eve, you're so pretty; I hate to see you looking so depressed. You're too blessed to be depressed...When I was your age my friends and I organized a secret society. The sisters of St. Joan. We stood in a circle and held hands, like this, and we swore to God and each other that all our lives we'd be like St. Joan. We'd devote ourselves to righting wrongs and being great. While other people became materialistic and dull, we would stay true; we would all be candles driving away the darkness of a cruel world. Well what do you think's happened to the brave sisters of St. Joan? Half of them are housewives who think they help the world by having supper ready on time. There's a grocery store assistant manager. A hack journalist. A city councilwoman implicated in campaign scandals. Their candles have all gone out, Eve. I'm the only one left. And as the only remaining Sister of St. Joan, I have the power to induct any new members I want. And I nominate for the sisterhood, Evening Star Hudson. If you choose to take the vow you will become a sister of St. Joan, but to become a sister, you have to accept the challenge. You have to say 'I do.' Do you, Evening Star Hudson, have the guts to be great?

Missing Pieces

Barbara Quintero

Scene: here and now

Serio-Comic
Judy: a philosophical lesbian, 40s

> *Judy's relationship with the vivacious and younger Lois is coming to an end. Realizing that a break-up is inevitable, Judy takes a moment to reflect on her life and her sexuality.*

JUDY: Well, I guess this is it, I can't take it anymore. This is it, a person only has so much patience. All the years of trying to hold on, trying to make it work, has exhausted me. It's time for me to move on, to start a new life, a better life. I don't see any other way of this working. I have to do this for my own survival, for my own sanity. I don't know. *(Pause.)* I don't think I asked for a lot in life. Did I? *(Pause.)* Did I want to be rich? Sure, who doesn't, but I accepted my working-class status, and mom's string of boyfriends; *(Aside.)* most of whom were always giving me the evil eye so I spent lots of time in my room hiding out, which led to my sketching, and painting and developed my artistic leanings, and a kind of nonchalance about the material world. No, obviously never money driven. I always knew I'd get by. Did I want to be better looking? Yeah, I did, but I convinced myself that talent and personality made up for not being beautiful. So, I'm okay about that. *(Pause.)* Did I want to be straight? Never. That's right, never! I accepted my role as dyke at a very young age. I went to work as a camp counselor at thirteen, thrown together in the woods with a hundred other budding prepubescent girls and their adolescent counselors. Everyone of them anxious to satisfy their raging hormones by experimenting sexually, some with boys, and some with girls. My first crush was on the lifeguard Diana. Diana, Diana, even the name made me swoon. Diana made me conscious of my sexual feelings. We would walk by the lake at night, the water had such a romantic effect on us, I knew I was in love, because it felt like a movie when we were together, not exactly real. The alcove where they stored the rafts was where I received my first kiss—and then there wasn't any doubt about who I was. Diana moved on to boys, but not me. *(Pause.)* Was I ashamed? No. It felt right. It was right. Right for me. I never really felt comfortable around guys. I'd seen enough jerks parading through my mother's life for years. The ones that ever tried to touch me were the worst, it would make my hair cringe at the thought of it. But none of them ever got very far—I'd boot them in the balls with a good karate chop, and let Mom know that it was time for a change. *(Pause.)* I knew I couldn't keep Lois with me forever. She's too young, and too free, too much like a bird flying from place to place. Not necessarily bad traits, in fact appealing, it's part of why I love her, and why, *(Pause.)* I know, I have to let her go.

Missing Pieces

Barbara Quintero

Scene: here and now

Serio-Comic
Lois: a young woman with a lust for life, 20s

> *Lois has been involved in a gay relationship but now wants to move on. Here, she describes her parents' unhappy existence, revealing the fear that keeps her moving from place to place and person to person.*

LOIS: Can you tell me, girlfriends, why I shouldn't be open to all sexual experiences—all that life has to offer. I mean, it's my life and what's the big deal anyway. I hate, Absolutely hate—all the hypocrisy in this world, I don't judge people, so why should any of them judge me. The damn Holy Rollers are the ones I hate the most. Those church-going hypocrites, so prim and pious—so outwardly perfect—all the while—all the while they're secretly fucking their brains out with whomever and whatever. Yup, even the clergy is sneaking into dirty little peep shows or bringing some young boy around to their rooms. They hide their sexual toys deep in their dresser drawer. If you ask me they are the ones to be afraid of—they are the really weird ones…I'm totally sane you see, because I'm comfortable with who I am, and what I do!—I only have one life, right!!! So, I'm not gonna miss out on any adventures of Any kind, that's fa sure, and I am definitely never ever going to hide who I am or what I do. Yeah, my folks were the epitome of those types I can't stand—so when I split fourteen, my mama's youngest—I promised myself to always live life upfront—and honestly, Yeah, corny as it sounds, true to myself, yeah I know, and go at life full speed. I sure didn't want to end up like my mama, that's fa sure— always stuck at home with us six kids. Yeah, Daddy was a minister, and yeah, I knew about the dirty picture collection in his private office. Oh, But he was proper to the core—and yes, mama was always one step behind him—always. *(Beat. She puts her hands together as if praying.)* Thank you mom—God bless your soul, mom. *(End praying.)* Yeah a minister's wife. Church and prayers were a daily requirement. And, you know what, I might have bought the whole package, the whole damn package, if I didn't recognize the facade at a very early age and if I didn't see the deadness in my mama's eyes or smelled the liquor on her breath. She kept her secret stash in the laundry room behind the bleach. Soon she was drinking herself into oblivion. Most days, by the time I came home from school, she'd be in bed already. "What's the matter, Ma?", I'd say, acting like I didn't know. "Oh Lo, Lo," she'd say to me, "I'm so sick, please start the dinner up. Sure, Ma, sure, where is everybody?" She'd pull the covers almost over her head, "coming back soon, better hurry baby." *(Beat.)* She looked so different in the pictures of her as a young girl—before she married Dad, at eighteen. A school teacher's daughter, she looked so beautiful, so open and peaceful. Full of life, I was told. Even in the pictures, a mischievous quality was in her eyes then, an anticipation. She was anxious, anxious for life and all that meant to her: family, teaching, love, marriage, and children. The whole shabang. *(Beat.)* So she did it. She led a respectable life; a minister's wife. Dogmatic and structured, never any variation, any change at all. There was just church, teaching Sunday school and keeping us kids perfect looking. On the outside, everything was perfect. All outward appearances of serenity, morality and perfection. The whole equation for happiness. But, I knew that mama wasn't really contented, I knew she was really dead inside, that look in her eyes, her diminished spirit, and I knew by the time I was ten years old that no way was I going to end up like her. Oh yeah, and Mom was dead at forty-two. *(Beat.)* I was twelve.

Mr. Melancholy

Matt Cameron

Scene: a desolate lighthouse

Dramatic
Dolores: a circus clown who has washed ashore at the lighthouse,
20–30

> *Dolores has come to care for Ollie, the misanthropic light-*
> *house keeper. When she tries to return to her life in the cir-*
> *cus, she discovers that she misses Ollie. She then returns to*
> *the lighthouse to confront Ollie with her feelings. Here, she*
> *finally washes off her clown makeup.*

DOLORES: The thing about clown makeup is you only ever have one
face. It never cracks, never drops, it's the face everyone wants to
see. Leave it on, I'm always a clown, I'm always happy…I wanted to see my face, underneath. So I wiped the clown away. *(Pulls
out a cloth from her pocket.)* I ran away to the circus the other
night…again. Deja vu. Never experienced deja—oh, you know
that routine. I missed the circus. The smell of the canvas, the
lightness of the cotton candy, the hum of the highwire stretched
taut overhead. Thought the circus missed me. But happiness goes
on without you, Ollie. It doesn't wait. It just goes on and you join
up with it or you don't…I couldn't even do the routines anymore.
Simple routines. Slapstick. I was missing one of my clown shoes
and I was being a bad clown. Children were crying. And for the
first time, the circus seemed to me a sort of sad place…and this
face seemed a sort of sad face.

Molly Sweeny
Brian Friel

Scene: Ireland

Dramatic
Molly Sweeny: a woman who has been blind since birth, 30s

> *Here, Molly describes her father's efforts to help her to "see" the world.*

MOLLY: By the time I was five years of age, my father had taught me the names of dozens of flowers and herbs and shrubs and trees. He was a judge and his work took him all over the county. And every evening, when he got home, after he'd had a few quick drinks, he'd pick me up in his arms and carry me out to the walled garden. "Tell me now," he'd ask. "Where precisely are we?" "We're in your garden." "Oh, you're such a clever little missy!" And he'd pretend to smack me. "Exactly what part of my garden?" "We're beside the stream." "Stream? Do you hear a stream? I don't. Try again." "We're under the lime tree." "I smell no lime tree. Sorry. Try again." "We're beside the sundial." "You're guessing. But you're right. And at the bottom of the pedestal there is a circle of petunias. There are about twenty of them all huddled together in one bed. They are—what?—seven inches tall. Some of them are blue-and-white, and some of them are pink, and a few have big, red, cheeky faces. Touch them." And he would bend over, holding me almost upside down, and I would have to count them and smell them and feel their velvet leaves and their sticky stems. Then he'd test me. "Now, Molly. Tell me what you saw." "Petunias." "How many petunias did you see?" "Twenty." "Color?" "Blue-and-white and pink and red." "Good. And what shape is their bed?" "It's a circle." "Splendid. Passed with flying colors. You *are* a clever lady." And to have got it right for him and to hear the delight in his voice gave me such pleasure. Then we'd move on to his herb bed and to his rose bed and to his ageratum and his irises and his azaleas and his sedum. And when we'd come to his nemophila, he always said the same thing. "Nemophila are sometimes called Baby Blue Eyes. I know you can't see them but they have beautiful blue eyes. Just like you. You're my nemophila." And then we'd move on to the shrubs and the trees and we'd perform the same ritual of naming and counting and touching and smelling. Then, when our tour was ended, he'd kiss my right cheek and then my left cheek with that old-world formality with which he did everything; and I loved that because his whiskey breath made my head giddy for a second. "Excellent!" he'd say. "Excellent testimony! We'll adjourn until tomorrow." Then if mother were away in hospital with her nerves, he and I would make our own meal. But if she were at home she'd appear at the front door—always in her headscarf and Wellingtons—and she'd shout, "Molly! Daddy! Dinner!" I never heard her call him anything but Daddy and the word always seemed to have a mocking edge. And he'd say to me, "Even scholars must eat. Let us join your mother." And sometimes, just before we'd go into that huge, echoing house, sometimes he'd hug me to him and press his mouth against my ear and whisper with fierce urgency, "I promise you, my darling, you aren't missing a lot; not a lot at all. Trust me." Of course I trusted him; completely. But late at night, listening to mother and himself fighting their weary war downstairs and then hearing him grope his way unsteadily to bed, I'd wonder what he meant. And it was only when I was about the same age as he was then, it was only then that I thought—I thought perhaps I was beginning to understand what he meant. But that was many, many years later. And by then mother and he were long dead and the old echoing house was gone. And I had been married to Frank for over two years. And by then, too, I had had the operation on the first eye.

Naked Mole Rats
In The World Of Darkness

Michael T. Folie

Scene: the Bronx Zoo

Serio-Comic
Barbara: a woman visiting the zoo with her family, 30–40

> *Here, Barbara is inspired by one of the zoo's denizens to make a telling observation about sex and monogamy.*

BARBARA: *(On a park bench. Reading from a zoo brochure/map.)* "Naked mole rats in the World of Darkness." The children will like that. Don't you think? *(Pause.)* They're alright by themselves? Aren't they? In the Children's Zoo? All by themselves? *(Pause.)* You're right. Of course they are. I mean, where can they go? How can they hurt themselves? That's what's so nice about the Children's Zoo. It's nature. But it's safe. *(Pause.)* Listen to this. "Naked mole rats live their entire lives under the ground. Furless and nearly blind, they experience the entire cycle of life—are born, grow up, mate, give birth and die—without ever seeing the light of day." *(Pause.)* I was reading in the *Times* the other day about prairie voles. They mate for life. And the males are like totally P.C. They don't screw around. They share equally in taking care of the offspring. It's because they secrete something. Some enzyme. The males do. *(Pause.)* Hah! You could sure make a fortune selling that stuff! Genuine Prairie Vole Anti-Asshole Fluid. You know how I'd market it? I'd put it in six-packs. Like beer. Make it appealing to the guys who need it most. See? I've learned a few things from you about packaging. *(Pause.)* And you say I never listen to you when you talk about work.

No Mean Street

Paul Boakye

Scene: an inner city

Dramatic
Jean: a woman confronting her HIV-positive lover, late 20s

> *When her estranged lover, Arlington, demands to see their eleven-year-old son, Jean angrily refuses, citing her reasons, her anger and her fear.*

JEAN: No Judge in his right mind is gonna let you anywhere near him. I'm the working one here, the almost qualified Social Worker, I'm the one constant thing in Marcus's life all these years. Where've you been? Fucking your way to AIDS?

[ARLINGTON: Bitch!]

JEAN: *(Chuckles.)* Names can't hurt me, Arlington. You done that. In just one fell swoop you managed to turn upside down everything I've accepted all my life. But I bet you never thought you were doing me a favor. It's never too late to change. I know that now. But when it came out, and you told me about this AIDS, yes, I exploded. I blamed it all on you. But it's up to me to protect my own body. It's up to me to take responsibility for my life. And I'll never go back to what I was. I felt hopeless for years living in this flat but now I've got hope. And if I die tomorrow, I'll never lose that. I used to worry about being lonely. Not having a man in my life. But not now. Now I feel I'm in control. So you do what you have to do. And I'll do what I have to do.

Portrait Of The Virgin Mary Feeding The Dinosaurs

Jeff Goode

Scene: the home of Mary and Joseph

Serio-Comic
The Virgin Mary

> *Here, Mary lectures her famous son about the power of the media.*

MARY: Son, history puts words in your mouth. Look, who said, "I cannot tell a lie"?

[JESUS: George Washington.]

MARY: *Wrong!* George Washington's *biographer* said, "I cannot tell a lie." George Washington never said it. He never chopped down a cherry tree. He lied to his father *all* the *time*. But history likes a good story, and now the cherry tree is just as real as his wooden teeth. You wanna hear a prophecy? What if I told you that 2000 years from now an overweight woman who looks nothing like me, in a dress I wouldn't be caught dead in, will sit in front of thirty* morons, claiming to be me, ranting and spouting language that would make me spin in my grave, that would make me blush to hear it—*if* I understood English, which I *don't*. And what if I said she'll do this: *(She does something uncharacteristic.)* And this: *(Does something else.)* And what if I said she'd do this: *(Does a handspring.)* And what if I told you her name was… *(She grabs a program out of the audience and reads the name of the actor playing Mary.)* …Daniele O'Loughlin. You'd say it was preposterous! *(Points at audience.)* They'll say it was prophecy! "That Virgin Mary?" they'll say, "what a woman! I used to think she was milquetoast, but now I have new insight! Now I understand her a little better! Now, after seeing this travesty, I think I like her! She had spunk. And what a visionary! Her prophecies were so accurate! Down to the letter! Did you know she predicted the crucifixion?"

[JESUS: *(Flabbergasted.)* I—I don't know what to say.]

MARY: Then shut up and eat your Cheerios.

* *use size of the audience as number*

Portrait Of The Virgin Mary Feeding The Dinosaurs

Jeff Goode

Scene: the home of Mary and Joseph

Serio-Comic
The Virgin Mary

> *As she does the ironing, Mary carps about her thankless role as messianic mom.*

MARY: Someone oughta write a book about me…They could call it *The Woman Behind the Man.* But then you could say that about every woman. Maybe they should call it that. *Everywoman.* Heck, let's not be sexist, you can call it *Everyman. Everyman: The Virgin Mary Story.* No, no it's definitely a woman thing. You don't see Joseph in here ironing the Messiah's underwear. He's out building a toolshed. Not for the Messiah. For himself. He wants a toolshed, so he builds one. I want a new dress, so I iron the clothes. Do you think I *want* to be ironing the clothes? You think I need this much underwear? *Men's* underwear? I don't *need* this. *(Picks up a pair of underwear.)* I don't need this. *(Picks up a pair of Bermuda shorts.)* I don't need one of these. *(Picks up a sweatshirt.)* I need one of these, but this one's too big for me. I don't need this one. I don't need any of this! Joseph wants a new toolshed, Joseph builds a new toolshed. Mary wants a new toolshed. Mary irons clothes. Mary asks Joseph for a new toolshed, Joseph says, "Not now, I'm building my own toolshed." Mary asks Jesus for a new toolshed, Jesus says, "Mom, I'm the Savior of Mankind. I don't know anything about construction work. " What did you learn from your father?? I could build a toolshed. If I had the time I don't even want a toolshed… *(She notices something in the pile of laundry.* What the…? *(Calling offstage.) Jesus Emmanuel Christ! Get in here! (Enter Jesus.)* What is this?

The Red Room

S. P. Miskowski

Scene: a farm in rural Georgia

Dramatic
Alma: a woman haunted by memories of the past, 30–50

> *Here, Alma shares a memory of her mother, Ruth, a killer executed by the state of Georgia.*

ALMA: *(Referring to a pair of long gloves Louise holds up for her inspection.)* No. Mother doesn't like those. *(Louise reluctantly puts them away. Alma speaks to Louise.)* I came home from school once, in October—the smell o dyin leaves in the air. Yellow and red. Only October has that smell, sharp as a needle. I ran up the porch steps. Screen door slammed shut behind me. But not the oak door. Later, I'd recall how the screen door slammed, but not the oak door. I was out o breath. "Mother!" I yelled. "I ran all the way home!" My face was hot. Sweat made my dress stick to my skin. "Mother!" No answer…I went to her room. The door was open. On the bed, her green dress was spread out, with black, emerald earrings placed where they would be if a woman was lyin on the bed in the dress and jewelry. Mother's green dress was waitin for her. "Mother!" *(She speaks to the audience. Alma crosses from behind scrim, toward center, as Louise crosses behind scrim. Louise faces upstage, wildly waving a scarf as Alma continues.)* I heard Louise, laughin. Outside! She wasn't supposed to go outside. I ran out, followin the sound, that's like water splashin, that wild way she laughs. I ran past the magnolia tree. Louise had her hair down round her face, pushin it around like somethin crazy, and laughin at me. I tried to catch ahold o her, but she got loose, and I fell down the bank, scratched my hands breakin my fall. Louise ran down the road. I was yellin at her, and runnin after. "Louise!"

[LOUISE: I liked to run!]

ALMA: "Come back in the house!"

[LOUISE: I could run fast. I could *run!*]

ALMA: Past Annie Swann's farm. Parted curtains. The door cracked open. "Look at that! The child! The sickly one. Look! Runnin down the road!"

[LOUISE: Look! Look! The sickly one!]

ALMA: I reached out, caught the tail o her blouse and it snapped out o my hand. She went rollin sideways down in the ditch. I caught up, pushed and kicked her 'til she stood up. Spun her around.

[LOUISE: Cut my arm. You hurt me.]

ALMA: "Shut up!" I pushed her ahead o me, all the way back home. Past Annie Swann's curtains and doors. Away from Annie Swann's pasture. Up the broken porch steps. Louise ran down the hall, cryin like some baby. Slammed the door o her room. Then *she* was there, middle o the hallway, starin at me. *(Alma puts hands on hips, taking on the shape of Mother. Louise emerges from behind scrim, listening.)* In her green dress and black emerald earrings, hands on her hips. Her black beads sparkled. She'd made up her face; her mouth was a dark line with no expression to it. She let one hand drop, and her fingers just-folded. No gloves.

[LOUISE: Mother doesn't like those.]

ALMA: "I found her, she didn't run far!" Could barely say, out o breath, chokin my words. Her hand reached up reached up—and slapped me hard across my mouth. And I tasted blood, sweet. And. She checked the clasps of her earrings.

[LOUISE: She was goin out.]

ALMA: *(To Louise.)* The next day, the first bee box was delivered before Mother came home.

The Red Room

S. P. Miskowski

Scene: a farm in rural Georgia

Dramatic
Martha: a woman haunted by memories of the past, 30–50

> *Martha's mother died in the electric chair. Now, she and her sisters, Alma and Louise share the family farm where all three struggle to cope with demons from the past. Here, Martha shares a dream.*

MARTHA: My dream used to come every few weeks. I don't know when it started, only I'd wake up screamin, afraid to sleep again. I was always ridin a bicycle down the far slope o the road goin home—when night started to fall. I'd try to ride faster, fightin the hill with my whole body 'til I couldn't breathe, and the hill rollin toward me and gettin higher at the same time. The faster I went, the faster the dark would fall, so by the time I was up the hill I couldn't see houses anymore, just their black shadows on the sides o me. Fast, fast, I rode to my house finally and got off my bicycle. The porch was dark, no lights in the window. Mother had forgot about me. Put out all the lights and gone to bed with me still outside. Then I saw the oak door was open partway, and I pushed on inside. Now the house all around me was thin and black as ink, so I couldn't tell which way was which. Cold! I put out my hands to feel my way but there was nothin to feel. I tried to call, "Mother! I'm downstairs. Come get me!" But my voice was dried up. Cool and sharp, somethin brushed past me. I heard a squeak like a rockin chair, steady. Cool rush again, on the other side of me. And kept on, creakin here and there, someplace in the dark. Then there was enough—just enough—just enough!— light so I could make out a shape as it brushed past me—there was all at once just enough light!—so I could see the sound and

78

the cool rush was comin from all around and up over me, where Mother and Louise and Alma were strung up on ropes, their bodies cut and bleedin, their bodies cut open, swingin past me with a cold rush back and forth, touchin me.

(*Louise and Martha address one another, though they do not look at one another.*)

[LOUISE: Wake up!]

MARTHA: I started to scream.

Romancing Oblivion

Steven Tanenbaum

Scene: here and now

Dramatic
Juliette (Jules): a restless spirit, 30s

> *Jules has been haunted by her sister's ghost since she was*
> *five. In an effort to atone for her part in her sister's death,*
> *Jules and her best friend, Alexandra, have taken several road*
> *trips which have turned into spiritual quests, the most recent*
> *of which landed the women in New Orleans. Unfortunately*
> *for Jules, the Big Easy is to be her final destination in this life.*
> *Here, her spirit describes coming to New Orleans and her*
> *death.*
>
> *(Lights come up on Jules. She is encircled in a halo of illumi-*
> *nation that is surrounded by complete darkness.)*

JULES: Now that all my time is spent rewinding events; it is clear
that the most obvious points of demarcation were the road trips.
Especially the last one. Yeah, New Orleans was definitely the
highlight. On that particular night, we went to see Boozoo
Chavis, this old-time Zydeco accordion player, who has a barn
outside of New Orleans that's been converted into a dance hall.
Alex and I were really determined to get into the flavor of the
place; so I did my part by knocking back Cajun martinis all night
long, and Alex held up her end by buying out the souvenir stand.
You see, Mrs. Boozoo, who's pushing eighty, sells these really
cheesy panties with the names of Mr. Boozoo's songs written on
the front of them. Alex bought two dozen pair that said "Play
with My Poodle." Anyway, by the time midnight rolled around, I
was getting pretty woozy from the martinis, so I decided to step
out for some fresh air. It was a glorious night and the air smelled

so sweet, just like you would expect it to in the South. I think I was still in the throes of some sort of nocturnal enchantment, when that Good Ol' Boy approached me. We started to talk—God knows what I said—but I remember him asking me if I wanted to take a ride in his pickup. Normally, I would never dream of doing such a thing, but he had really soft eyes; and between the martinis and the air, I was positively intoxicated. Besides, just at that precise moment when the opportunity presented itself for me to hesitate and think better of his proposal, the wind picked up and caressed my ears with its sweet exhalations. I could swear it was whispering, "Yes," just to me. So, the next thing I can remember, we're in his pickup truck and we're backing out of this embankment or something. I'm really not sure because it was pitch black outside. Then the truck got stuck in the mud so he stepped on the gas to give us a little push; and the next thing I know, we went flying right over the embankment, which caused the truck to flip over on its back, before landing in a shallow canal. The water was only about three feet high but the mud at the bottom of the canal prevented us from opening the doors. I remember looking at that Good Ol' Boy and we both kind of shrugged at each other as the water started to pour into the cab. It's not like I was counting or anything, but it took about forty minutes before we both drowned. At the very last moment, when the cab was almost completely filled with water and there was about ten seconds of oxygen left, I decided not to fight it any longer. So, I closed my eyes and took a very deep breath, letting the water rush into my lungs. It seemed as if I was being blown up with air like a balloon; and just when I felt like I had expanded beyond all possible limits, I burst apart. Or at least I thought I did. When I opened my eyes, I found myself in the same place that I'm in now. I've come to realize that this is the place that my sister's been whispering to me ever since she died. And now it will be from this place, that I will whisper to Alex.

Second Sunday In May

A. Giovanni Affinito

Scene: here and now

Dramatic
Janet: a woman confronting her aging mother, 40–50

> *Here, Janet reveals her fears about her daughter, Cory to her mother while challenging the older woman not to die.*

JANET: I don't have any answers for you moms. Here you are, maybe dying and you're agonizing over a few social snubs. So what can you do about it? Bring back the old days? Is that what you want?

[ANITA: My life is really over isn't it?]

JANET: That's up to you. Life, for me means a home, a family, a few good friends. We've got this little shop that's no big deal, but we make a living and we're happy in our way. But Cory, is so confused by this crazy world she never made, this loony bin she was born into, that she tries to find solace in bizarre cults, in exotic techniques to feel safe in a pretended world. I don't blame her. But sometimes, just sometimes I want to slap her very hard. Literally. I want to make her mad enough to break out of her dream and fight for a place where she can breath in the fullness and richness of her own existence.

[ANITA: My *God* Janet. What a women you are.]

JANET: Don't leave Moms, and don't die. You know what I think? When an old person dies, a whole library is destroyed.

Slaughter City

Naomi Wallace

Scene: Slaughter City, USA

Dramatic
Roach: a black woman who works at the slaughter house, 30s

> *Here, Roach remembers a time in her childhood when she felt special.*

ROACH: You remember Mr. Morton? Our second grade teacher? You used to get jealous 'cause he would take me fishing and he wouldn't ever take you.

[MAGGOT: I remember: teacher's pet.]

ROACH: Yeah, well, he liked fishing the way I liked it and sometimes after school he'd take me down to the stream. He was the first white man who ever treated me like a child likes to be treated. Like I had something special about me that only he could see. *(Beat.)* When Mr. Morton cast a good line, his ears would go red. Red as a worm.

[MAGGOT: *(Sings.)* Oh my love is like a red, red, worm.]

ROACH: They say a worm has seven hearts and that if you break it up in the right places, two or three of the pieces will live. Problem was, I never knew where the hearts were or where to put the hook in. That's why I mostly use artificials now. *(She casts her rod as if out into the audience and reels it back in.)* Switchback, rapalla, bass magnet, double-headed jig. Twelve-pound line. Eight-pound line. I was using a six-pound line that day and I landed a four-pound small-mouth bass. You remember the picture. That fish was longer than my arm! Almost snapped my line. Mr. Morton and I skinned it right there and cooked it over the fire. I can tell you I was proud that day. And Mr. Morton was proud of me too. He kissed me on the mouth four times, one kiss for each pound of that bass. Have you ever made your teacher that proud of you? I liked him better than my own Daddy because he took me fishing and my own father never had time because he was always at the packhouse splittin' hogs. *(Beat.)* Four times. On the mouth. He said he wanted to know what my kind…tasted like. *(Beat.)* That's how proud he was. That's how. Yes. And I closed my eyes because I had to. Because if a worm has seven hearts it could have eight and I wanted him to know I could take it. And I took it. Right there in the grass beside the stream. *(Beat.)* But once it's cut you never can tell just which parts of the worm have been killed and which parts will crawl away and start over because all of the parts are moving. All of the parts are trying to live. But only one or two of them do. Live. Funny. How you can look at a body and see nothing but the whole of it. But I know. I know which parts went on and lived and which parts gave up and died. Can you tell them apart? If you touch yourself, here and here? Go on. Try it. Can you tell just which parts of you are dead and which parts of you are still alive? *(Beat.)* Yeah. I know what it's like, Maggot. I just don't let it lead me. And you and me are lucky. Sure-all-to-hell-lucky that we still got parts of us that are alive. *(Beat.)* All right then? When you're ready? *(Beat.)* Damn it, Maggot. I should punch you in the mouth but—*(She hands Maggot the rod and Maggot takes it.)* it's the weekend and you and me are going fishing!

Smoke & Mirrors

Eric C. Peterson

Scene: here and now

Dramatic
Simone: a woman who has just discovered that she is HIV positive, 20–30

> *Simone has always allowed herself to be ruled by passion, both emotional and physical; an indulgence for which she must now pay the ultimate price.*

SIMONE: I lost my virginity when I was fourteen years old…but not the way most fourteen-year-olds would, in the back of an Oldsmobile with some sweaty football player who doesn't even know where your clitoris is, much less what to do with it… although I've had that experience, too…My virginity was stolen away by Mr. Henderson…my ninth-grade Biology teacher. Obviously, he taught me a lot more about Biology than just what was in our books. We did it after school, on top of his desk, with the door wide open. He liked it that way. He told me that sex…can either be because you love someone or just for fun, and that with us, it was just for fun. I said that I understood. He forgot to tell me that you could fall in love with the fun…He told me that it wouldn't hurt so much the second time, and it didn't…Last week, I was feeling a little dizzy, and my period was late, so…I went to the doctor to see if I might be pregnant. Saturday, I got a phone call from the clinic. My blood tests were—…Well, they couldn't tell me anything over the phone, but they needed to see me right away; Sunday would be fine, they said… *(Long pause.)* …I've got it. I've got it…I always told myself to live each day as if it were my last; I guess now I'll really mean it. God…I keep on thinking that this is some horrible nightmare and that tomorrow I'll wake up, and it will all be over. At the party last night…I noticed two men behind me...lovers. They looked so happy... together. I wanted so bad to feel what they were feeling, but...I couldn't. So I got drunk. I asked Tom to marry me. It used to be this game I would play on him whenever he got too pushy, but... last night I meant it. I thought that maybe if someone would marry me, I would be all clean and white again...like when I was fourteen years old. I'll never make love to anyone again. All I can do is remember...I can remember Tom...and I can remember boys in the back of their parents' Oldsmobiles, and...a tiny pearl of sweat falling from Mr. Henderson's mustache onto one of my breasts. Dammit...What am I going to do...? Oh, God...

The Souvenir Of Pompeii

Sari Bodi

Scene: here and now

Dramatic
Natalie: a woman who never tries too hard because she's happy right where she is, 30s

> *When Natalie's neighbor, Helen, kidnaps another woman's baby from the hospital, reporters waste no time in beating a path to her door. Here, pragmatic Natalie fields their questions.*

NATALIE: Yeah, I knew her. She was my next-door neighbor, wasn't she. And I could have told you this would happen, too. I knew she'd steal a baby. I would have called the police if her husband hadn't. I could see her staring at my four kids like she wished they were hers. And just think, I let her hold my littlest one, too. You know, just so she could get her hormones flowing and have one of her own. But she's the type that'll probably never have a kid. She's too skinny. You gotta have some fat on you to produce babies. That's a fact. Yeah, I knew she'd do something like this. She read too much. Whenever I stopped over her house to show her my kids, and let her touch them and stuff, she'd be reading some book on ancient civilizations. Then she'd tell me how women in Greek society didn't have any status. I mean, who cares? She should come to my house and see how much status I got. But I could see how she felt like a failure. I mean conceiving a kid is probably one of the easiest things you'll ever do in your life. You know I'm sure she got A's on all her papers in school, and I got C's, but hey in the test on populating the universe, she's now getting an F. Like I said, it never pays to be an over-achiever. It's a much happier place in the middle. I kept telling her, you want one of these babies like I got, then stop reading those books and relax. I mean I've only ever read three books all the way through and look at all the kids I have. Number one was *The Bridges of Madison County,* of course. But you couldn't show your face at a Tupperware party in this neighborhood if you hadn't read that. Number two was *Women Who Love Too Much,* well, cause that's me. But my absolute favorite is still *Gone with the Wind.* Sometimes at night when all the kids are sleeping, and Glen is snoring so I really can't sleep, I'll pretend that this house is Tara and that Glen has all his hair and is Rhett Butler. You know, I don't tell my kids about this Scarlett O'Hara stuff because I don't want them to be encouraged by dreams. Dreams are very harmful. I mean it's very unlikely—probably a million to one chance of one of them becoming president, so why give them false hopes. But they're healthy kids. And you know why? It's because I breast fed each one of them till they were two years old. It was a sacrifice cause sometimes it looked a little funny to have one of them walk up to me and take a suck, but...Hey, do you want to see them? They're probably the healthiest kids you'll ever see. Oh, okay, well then some other time. No, I don't know where she is. I'm certainly not hiding her here. I think a woman who takes a mother's baby should be shot. She doesn't respect the birth process. And I'd tell her that to her face. Well, I tell you, when Glen and I were watching the television last night and saw her picture on the news, it was the most surprised I ever saw Glen. Well, we'd never known a celebrity before. So Glen says to me, "See I told you she was crazy." And of course he never did but he always likes to be right about people. So I said, "No, Glen, I told you she was going crazy, but you never listen to me." And he says, "No, I'm the one that spotted it." So we went back and forth like this, until it suddenly came to me. Here is a chance to use my all-time favorite line, so I sat back in my chair, pushed my dinner away, and said, "Frankly, my dear, I don't give a damn." So I won the argument. Which I have to say was one of the most fun moments of my marriage.

The Souvenir Of Pompeii

Sari Bodi

Scene: here and now

Dramatic
Jennifer: a young woman whose baby has just been stolen from the hospital, 20s

> *Here, desperate Jennifer demands to be released from the hospital so she may search for her kidnapped child.*

JENNIFER: Please, don't give me any more Valium. I promise I won't scream. I'm the only one who can find my baby. The smell of her is imbedded in my nose. I could track her down like a foxhound. A whale swallowed my baby. A whale disguised as a doctor came into this hospital room, and gulped her down like a piece of algae. I was the rock that Molly was perched on. And I gave way to the whale. I know. I didn't deserve to be a rock. No, get away from me with that shot. I'm calm. You saw Molly when she first came out of me, looking just like a little wet chicken. Did you see her eyes? She has a tiny piece of detached cornea floating in her right eye. Dr. Harding probably saw it as a handicap in a society that screams for perfection in the beauty of its women. But I took it as a sign that she is destined to see the world differently than most children. She will be an observer, perhaps a writer, like me. Oh, I should never have let Dr. Harding cut the umbilical cord. Then no matter where she was right now, even inside the belly of a whale, I could give a tug and she would come flying back to me. And I would lick her all over like a mother dog her puppy, and steal millions of spider's webs to wrap her up so tightly she could never leave me again. I told you. I don't want any more medication. And I don't want you to feel sorry for me. Sympathy is overrated. It's one of those pretend emotions, like romantic love. Molly was born out of need, and lust and longing for a seed in my belly. Not romantic love. It was very deliberate. Please get me my clothes, and take me out of here. I tell you, they need my nose.

The Split

Jack Gilhooley and Jo Morello

Scene: NYC

Serio-Comic
Marie Rossini Williamson: highly successful playwright, 40–60

> *Marie and her husband, Charlie are a winning writing team who have recently separated. Here, Marie describes her lonely new single life to her agent.*

MARIE: Every morning. I read the greeting cards at the mall for laughs. Then off to lunch.

[RICKIE: The country club? With a date?]

MARIE: McDonald's. Alone. Then I come home and channel-surf the talk shows in search of a dramatic theme. Something sensitive, plausible, humane. No dice. The mail arrives. I clip and paste the contest labels. Why not, for ten million dollars? Should I choose the red Jaguar or the black Mercedes? I send the NRA questionnaire to the ACLU. I stuff the Christian Coalition material into the Americans For Democratic Action envelope. A telephone solicitor calls. *(Mimicking.)* "How ya doin, Mrs. Williams?" So, I tell her. I tell her it's Williamson, not Williams. But it would be Rossini except for the outmoded marital customs in this country. I tell her about the deeply entrenched male-female double standard in America. I tell her about my play which explores this injustice from the perspective of an Italian-American family in Dayton, Ohio. I'm about to ask her if she'd like to read a copy. But she's hung up.

The Sweet By 'n' By

Frank Higgins

Scene: Glen Daniel, West Virginia, a coal mining town

Dramatic
Babe: the outspoken widow of a coal miner, 40–50

> *Babe is obsessed with getting her daughter, Libby, out of
> Glen Daniel. She is determined that Libby won't know the
> same kind of life that she's lived in their insular community.
> When she convinces a childhood friend of Libby's to convince
> the girl to go to college, her motives are questioned by her
> mother and best friend. Here, she does her best to explain
> her feelings.*

BABE: Newton n me worked it all out. He's just gonna tell her
there's better things in life than Glen Daniel, West Virginia.

[GRAMMA: You got on perfume. He spose to talk better if you
smell better?]

BABE: You both shut up. You member goin to the mass funeral for
our husbands, Geneva? Sure you do, you was there lookin like
you'd been hit over the head. N the organ were playin "We Shall
Understand It Better By n By."

[GRAMMA: I member.]

BABE: While all of you was cryin n prayin, I sat there n imagined all
the people who ever died, after they knock themselves out down
here they git up to Heaven, n Jesus shows 'em the Book of Life
with all the answers in it, n all the people worn down by this
world nod their heads n say, 'I shoulda known, I woulda turned
here 'stead of there, I woulda been happier.' N I sat at that funeral thinkin, "Is all this religion stuff true? Is God really gonna give
us the answers in the sky? Are we really gonna understand it better by n by? When it's too late?" I decided right then I would *not*
let my daughter live the same kind of life I had. I would not let

91

her be somebody who thinks she's livin good if she lives in a house with wallpaper. Now I got Newton comin for one reason only, to tell her bout college n the world n that's *it*. If the two of you don't like it, you can both dig a hole to Hell n climb in.

Texans Do Tap Dance

Richard Lay

Scene: New York City

Dramatic

Samantha: a young woman desperate to hang on to her boy-friend, 20s

> *When Billy decides to go home to Texas following college graduation, pregnant Samantha begs him to stay without revealing her secret.*

SAMANTHA: Good luck Billy, I'll light a candle for you every night. Will I ever see you again?

[BILLY: If you don't blow out the candle.]

SAMANTHA: I haven't got anything left but to beg you…beg you not to go. Beg you to stay. Begging you Billy. That's what I'm doing. *(Beginning to cry.)* I don't know what else to do. I can't live without you…I know it. I can't threaten you. I can't do *anything* to you. I just want you…Remember when we camped behind the dunes that first summer. Remember we put the tent up and the wind got wild and the waves rushed over the dunes and the tent floated away and we just cling to each other and laughed and you said "why don't we just die together." The way you said it you meant it, like we were the most important people in the world…that our fate was bigger than anything that had ever existed. *(Still teary.)* The sound of the waves and that terrible wind blocked out almost everything. And we slid across the sands in our wind-proofed tent with its attached blue plastic bottom and your laughter muffled the fear and our love *was* forever. Remember? *(Laughing now.)* And you remember when you said you wanted twins and we went into the baby shop and picked out pink and blue everything—not to buy but to feel. I could smell our twins and see them smile. It was like we had our babies. Oh Billy *(Sobbing.)* we had so much.

[BILLY: Poor Sam.]

SAMANTHA: *(Sniffing.)* I am beyond begging. I'm beyond everything. I am beyond myself. We made love two hundred and thirty eight times…Yes, I did count. That as to give me some credit in your future.

Texans Do Tap Dance

Richard Lay

Scene: New York City

Serio-Comic
Ma: woman of the world, Texas-style, 50–60

> *Here, an earthy ex-tart provides details of her life as a hooker in suburban Texas.*

MA: In my day I was the best hooker these parts has ever seen! Most of them tarts from the North would index their Johns by numbers. *(Sniff.)* I always did mine by colors. Like red was very important. Blue was romantic but married. Green was, well you know green…maybe rich. Yella was the sheriffs' sons. They'd screw me then arrest me *(Pause.)* then apologize. Black, well speaks for itself. White was freebies…the colors went on and on. Times were good. How I didn't get pregnant is a miracle. And then the Lord smiled and I was…with Lorraine-Jane. I always promised myself that if I had a baby I would stop working. My ma was on the game too and she didn't stop when I was on the way and she gave *me* away to the Salvation Army, who took me in and raised me. They taught me the trumpet and I became Miss Salvation Army Band Girl of 19…whatever it was. They put me in the fish cannery when I was fifteen. I only lasted two days. I walked out smelling of damn mackerel and the Sally Army—who can be mean if you don't behave—kicked me out and said they would sing for my redemption. So I followed in my mother's footsteps. When I got with a baby I just gave up the game and ran into Charlie. My Charlie used to be a pasteurized milk salesman. He got laid off and his sister in Mexico invited him down there to cheer him up. Course, he had to get a passport…but he only had enough space to write pastor *(Pause.)* on the application form… so he became one. He's been a good daddy to Lorraine-Jane. And he's a good pastor too. People call him reverend…but I know that deep down he still misses selling pasteurized milk and chewing the cud with farmers about beef prices. Lorraine-Jane calls him daddy and he taught her how to dance and act, cos he used to be with a carnival. Why, he'd bounce her on his knee until she was eighteen…and they'd be laughing and cuddling. He calls her Sugar and she calls him Pops. We are a *happy* family.

Twinges From The Fringe

Bob Jude Ferrante

Scene: here and now

Serio-Comic
Myrna: an actress, 20s

> *Myrna came to New York City with one burning ambition: to become a hooker. Here, she tells the story of how she was side-tracked into acting.*
>
> *(Music: Cool, smoky jazz music, like, heavy sax action. Myrna comes out in a trench coat and spiked heels. She lights and drags heavily on a cigarette, blows the smoke out over the audience.)*

MYRNA: Myrna. Myrna Flotzkengruschnimmer. You heard my name before. And my story. Small town—Cole's drugs. Greyhound depot. A big door waiting to open. Worked at Cole's two years. That's a lot of Tampax. But I had this big dream—to be a hooker. Day finally comes I buy the ticket, get on that Greyhound to Fun City. My whole nest egg goes for an apartment. I pound the pavement, try to learn the biz. Nights, I hang out in hotel lobbies, dream of getting discovered, like Margo St. James. The men. Not interested. They go, "Get lost, we see hundreds of broads like you every day." Sometimes I get close. But one guy goes, "Your legs are too long," another, "I don't like the shape of your face." Six months, bammo, nest egg's gone. That's a lot of Tampax. Living on nail-clippings. Out on Bowery, looking for some. This guy. A hungry look, up, down; goes, "Sweetheart, buy you dinner?" I go, "Sure." What the hell, girl's gotta eat. I say, "I'm trying to break into prostitution." He goes, "Sweetheart! I'm a pimp! Rosa Vindaloo, six P.M., we'll eat, discuss it." I go home, get dolled up. Thinking, "Be careful girl, *says*

97

he's a pimp, maybe it's a line…" At six I'm there. Got it all: low-back outfit, fishnet stockings, hair up. The guy—Murray Steinoblatski—gets a table. Whispers in the waiter's ear. Waiter nods. Then: Cajun duck napolitan with capers. And wine. Should be careful—can't hold my liquor. But two bottles later, I spill it, life story: Flat on my back 'cause I can't get flat on my back. He goes, "Let me help. I got equipment. I'll get you started in pro business." We leave Rosa's, get in his Jag. Street lights whip by, mind's racing: "Is this finally it—the big break?" But we get there: no equipment. Stanislavski teacher, voice coach Murray's an *agent!*—it's a *put-up job!* Coat's not even off, they break out the hard stuff—Pinter, Miller, Shaw. I can see it coming. But two apes hold me down. And Steinoblatski…bastard…forces me to…*act.* *I,* who always thought "Mark Taper Forum" a simple request for help with bondage. Can't believe it! Want to *rip* that smile off his smug face. But then, we're doing *The Homecoming* "'e finks 'e knows about horses'." there's this sensation…*down there.* I got a—maybe it's sick?—*through line.* When it's over, Murray says, "Kid, you're a natural." I run to the bathroom to throw up. I'm turned out. Uta's teaching me about French scenes. Cicely's got me breathing from the diaphragm. Big bucks. Murray says, once you see Myrna's head shot, you'll never cast another. Plush. First there's guilt. But a girl's gotta pay the rent. I'm resigned to the life. Doing *Henry IV,* Part II next Tuesday on *Great Performances.* But you know the story. Can't save a goddamned dime in Fun City.

Wait

Brian Christopher Williams

Scene: a restaurant

Serio-Comic
Edna: a woman planning to leave her husband, 30s

> *Here, Edna announces her intention to leave her husband and start a new life.*

EDNA: —It's not yours. I was going to wait until Linda and Larry arrived before I told you. I wanted someone here to console you, but I just can't stand the pressure another minute.

[JACK: Wait. This is going too fast.

EDNA: That's just it, Jack. I couldn't wait another minute. I'm forty-four years old. If I didn't act now, it would be too late. I visited a sperm bank, Nobel prize winners. I'm going to hatch an egghead, Jack. You'd find out anyway; it'll show up on your credit card bill. Oh, that reminds me, these are yours now. American Express, American Express Gold, Optima, Visa, Visa Gold, Carte Blanche, Diners Club, Discover (Nobody takes that one anyway.), another Visa, Mastercharge, MCI, and six or seven department stores. I hope you don't mind. I had to buy a few things for the new place.

[JACK: Edna, what are you—]

EDNA: —Oh, that's right, I didn't tell you. Whoops. Sorry. Breach of etiquette. I'm leaving you. I'm going to hibernate for a few months until I hatch; then, I don't know. Maybe I'll find myself a lesbian lover and live on a commune. We'll see. I've got a future, Jack. *(Pause.)* Good-bye, Jack.

When Language Fails

Gail Noppe-Brandon

Scene: a hospital

Dramatic
Kate: a woman whose daughter has been brutally raped, 40–50

> *Lee has been in a state resembling catatonia since her rape and beating by a serial killer. Here, strong-willed Kate does her best to get her daughter to speak.*
>
> *(Kate sits beside Lee, who sits and stares straight out. Kate holds a teddy bear out to Lee.)*

KATE: Lee? Your friend Samantha called. I told her you were in the hospital. I said you had pneumonia...no one needs to know. *(Lee does not react, Kate indicates bear.)* She sent this. Do you want it? *(No answer. Kate retracts it.)* I didn't think you would. I told her you were a little beyond stuffed animals, but she said "No one's ever beyond stuffed animals." She insisted that I bring it. *(Silence.)* Should I leave it? *(She circles once or twice, observing Lee, then sits in the chair where Jeni had been sitting.)* Lee? *(Silence.)* What are you doing, Lee? *(Pause.)* You're breaking my heart. *(Kate starts to break, then recovers.)* I want you to stop this. This reign of silence. It's very childish, and it's accomplishing nothing. Lee? *(Silence.)* If you talk to anyone, it should be to me. You don't have to talk to the cop if you don't want to. I'd like to see the bastard that did this to you hung, but that's *her* problem. She can do her lousy job without you. *I* need you. I'm sitting out here in the dark, and you're all I have. *(She reaches out and touches Lee's cheek, Lee recoils.)* What is this, Lee? What kind of game are you playing here? Are you punishing me? *(Silence.)* A mother's just a human being. We can't keep our children safe from every terrible thing that can happen to them in this world.

We like to think we can, but we can't. *(Silence.)* Lee, you're frightening me. I don't know what to do here. You weren't willful like this as a little child. You were my sturdy little helper. *(Silence.)* You're a grown woman now Lee; you're starting college in a few months. *College.* You think this is how a college student behaves? *(Silence. Kate thinks about this, and concludes.)* You don't want to be a grown woman anymore. Is that it? *(Lee blinks.)* It's not easy Lee, *I* know. But you can't go backwards. That's why I raised you to be a *strong* woman. You screamed like I taught you, and he ran away. *(Lee starts to rock.)* Stop that rocking. Please, Lee.

(Lee doesn't, it has a very *disturbing effect on Kate.)*
Lee, do you want to end up in a booby-hatch? You want to throw away your whole life over this? You've got to pull yourself together Lee, that's the name of the game. *(Pause. Lee keeps rocking. After a beat, She reaches for Lee, tries to pull her up. Jeni enters the booth, where a fluorescent light comes up, she sits and watches, unbeknownst to Kate or Lee.)* I'm taking you out of here. *(Lee extricates herself, Kate stares at her.)* Don't you want to come home with me? Lee? *(Lee turns away from Kate in her chair—it is a "no". After a long silence, Kate sits.)* You know what men used to do to women, after they raped them? *(Silence.)* Cut their tongues out, Lee. So they couldn't talk. So they couldn't tell anyone who did it. *(Silence. Jeni looks away.)* You want to go back to the middle ages, Lee? *(Silence.)* I thought you were a *modern* woman. I thought you were a *feminist.* I thought you were my little warrior. You have to be strong now, Lee. I need you to be strong. I need you to tell me you're okay, Lee. Just tell me you're okay. *(Lee turns away, stops rocking. Kate breaking down again. She places teddy bear on floor—leans in—softly.)* Lee-Lee, remember after daddy died? I used to come home late from work, and you'd make dinner for me? You made me a lamb chop once, and you cooked it so long, it was black. Black like a piece of charcoal! And I ate it, all of it. *And* I told you it was delicious. Cause that's what you needed to hear. So I said it. Cause that's what love is about Lee. Sometimes you have to say what someone you

love needs to hear. I *need* to hear you say something now, Lee. *(She turns her back to Lee, giving her some privacy in which to begin talking. Lee reaches down and picks up the teddy bear, clutches it, rocks with it.)* Just three little words, Lee. *"I'm okay, Mom."* That's all I'm asking you for, Lee. It's not a lot to ask.

(Silence. After a beat Kate turns around, sees Lee rocking with the bear, moves upstage to her.) Stop this nonsense. *(Lee looks away. Kate just stares at Lee for a beat, then she squats beside her, puts her head on Lee's lap—her face to the audience—her head on the bear. She finally breaks down and cries. After a beat, Lee looks down at Kate, and then mechanically pats her head. Kate looks up at Lee hoping to make contact, but Lee has already averted her eyes. Kate stares at Lee for a beat, wipes her eyes and composes herself as best she can. She smoothes Lee's hair.)* I'm tired Lee. I'll see you tomorrow.

When Language Fails

Gail Noppe-Brandon

Scene: a hospital

Dramatic
Jeni: a frustrated cop, 30s

> *Jeni has been doing her best to encourage Lee, a victim of a brutal rape, to describe her attacker, a serial killer who has raped and murdered several other young women. Unfortunately, Lee remains in a catatonic state and refuses to speak. Here, Jeni dispenses with the mask of concerned police officer and speaks to Lee on a level she hopes will break through the terrified girl's defenses.*

JENI: Dr. Burt will be a few minutes late. *(Silence. Jeni studies Lee.)* Oh, Lee. *(Pause.)* I give up. I guess it's just all gone, isn't it. *(Lee lifts her head.)* The past, the present. *(Pause. Jeni removes her gun and walkie-talkie, slides them away in the opposite direction.)* Even if Jeni catches that man and locks him up, she'll be getting there too late for Lee. Cause he killed Lee, didn't he? Not the same way he killed those other girls, no. They don't have a chance for a *new* life. But I think he killed you, too. *(Lee starts to rock.)* Everybody wants Lee to talk, but maybe Lee is dead…And the dead can't talk. Jeni should know, cause Jeni's been there too. Yes indeed, Jeni knows exactly where you're at. *(Lee lifts her focus, but doesn't look at Jeni.)* I'm gonna tell you something. *(Pause. This is very hard for Jeni to say.)* My uncle raped me. I was eighteen, too. *(Pause. Lee is listening.)* My Mamma loved that old drunk. He used to dress up as Santa, at Christmastime. But drink can make people violent. *(She fingers her throat.)* When I finally told, at first she didn't want him to move out. He was all the family she had—he was never even punished. *(Looks at Lee for a moment.)* Maybe your Mamma can't *ever* have you back. You just can't be that old Lee anymore, Lee. Nope. She'll have to take the *new* Lee. The one who may not go on to college right away. The one who maybe won't want to date for a long time to come. The one who may not enjoy sex again—ever. The one whose not gonna be what everyone wants her to be anymore. The one whose gonna look sad and angry, a lot more than she's gonna look happy. *(Pause. Lee has stopped rocking.)* My name used to be "Joy". Yup. *(She laughs bitterly.)* Maybe we shouldn't call you *Lee* anymore. Maybe you're *After-Lee,* or *New-Lee.* Maybe the stuff Dr. Burt wants you to remember, doesn't even count, cause they're some other girl's memories. I don't know… *(Pause.)* Maybe even the rape happened to someone else. Maybe it happened to some sweet young girl who wouldn't have believed anyone would want to hurt her that way. Some girl whose lying out there alone on the street, waiting. Waiting for the people who cared about her, to come along and bury her. And say a prayer for her soul. And grieve for her. Grieve for the life she could have had, the other Lee, that someone came along and stole. *(Pause. Lee looks at her own hands—inert in her lap.)* I wanted to kill myself after I was raped. I should have wanted to kill *him,* but maybe I just wanted to be with the rest of me that was already dead… *(Jeni studies Lee.)* Maybe Jeni can help you bury that old Lee, so you can cry for her soul. *(Lee looks at her.)* You want Jeni to bury that old Lee, right here in Jeni's arms? *(Lee wants it, but doesn't respond. Jeni takes Lee in to her arms and rocks her. After a long beat, she sings.)*

"Precious Lord, take my hand, lead me on, help me stand.
I am tired, I am weak,
I have walked through the storms,
Through the night—
Lead me on, to the light.
Take my hand Precious Lord,
Lead me home…"

You want me to bury that old Lee, don't you baby.

When Starbright Fades...

Sandra Marie Vago

Scene: Augusta, Georgia, the early 1960s

Dramatic
Laura: a young woman trapped in an abusive marriage, 18

> *Laura's husband, Marty, is about to be shipped to Vietnam
> and has become increasingly violent as a result. Here, Laura
> confesses her dream to one day become an artist to her sym-
> pathetic neighbors.*

LAURA: I had a girlfriend once, went all the way to Las Vegas.

[MITZI: Las Vegas?]

LAURA: *(Excitedly.)* She told me! She said they got people out there
that draw pi'tures like I do and she said...they make money sell-
in' 'em to the tourists...the people stayin' in the hotels, ya know?

[MITZI: Is that right?]

LAURA: Oh, yeah, she said it's beautiful out there...the mountains,
the desert, the canyons. I bet it is too. All the lights and the people all spendin' money and laughin' 'n happy...The heat ain't so
bad there, either. She told me it's like a dry heat, the kind you
don't feel...I'll bet it's really nice there.

[MITZI: You oughtta draw pictures for money.]

LAURA: I just love to draw. *(Pause.)* One time I did one of Marty
without him knowin'...a surprise. He liked it too, he was real
proud of it! He liked to look at my drawin' back then. He hung it
on the wall and later on, he even took it to the base to show the
guys...A while later, some Lieutenant drew a mustache on it and
sign across the top sayin' "Wanted." Marty got mad and done
somethin'...He didn't wanna bring it home, he didn't want me to
know, he was afraid it'd hurt my feelings... *(Pause.)* Wadn't long
after that him'n that Lieutenant had another big fight,
over...somethin' else. But I know it all started cause'a me drawin' that pi'ture. *(She doesn't laugh.)* He stopped lookin' at my
drawing after that.

When Starbright Fades...

Sandra Marie Vago

Scene: Augusta, Georgia, the early 1960s

Dramatic
Laura: a young woman trapped in an abusive marriage, 18

> *Laura was sexually abused by her father when she was a small child. Here, she relates the events of a sadly parallel dream.*

LAURA: Ya know, this afternoon when I was here alone I was dreamin' this crazy dream. I was a little girl and I came home with a Robin redbreast I drew...it was one a those nights when daddy wadn't feelin' good. *(She giggles nervously, like a ten year old.)* All of a sudden, my mamma yelled, "Run, honeygirl!" *(She stops.)* Then daddy was yellin', how, now he hadda whip me cause mama yelled! It was really scary all of a sudden. He said he didn't like whippin' me, he just wanted to love me. He always wanted to just love me. *(She suddenly gets very quiet and almost frightened.)* He'd come up to my room, put his arms around me, hold me and lay next to me. I could hear him breathing...his heart beatin'...so close...He'd stay a long time. Then, he'd do the strangest thing. *(She laughs.)* He'd cry! Ain't that funny? I mean he'd hurt me and then *he'd cry...I* never did. *(She takes a pillow from her bed and cradles it like a baby. Mitzi starts to say something but Louella motions for her to be quiet and let Laura talk.)* I'd hear 'em later, him 'n mamma, downstairs yellin' 'n arguin' about it. Then, after awhile, they'd stop fightin' 'n they'd be doin', you know, that love stuff. I'd listen with my ear against the bottom of a glass...like I saw in a movie one time. I'd listen and I'd hear daddy snorin' and mamma cryin' all alone down there in the dark. That's when I'd say, I hate you mamma. I don't know why, but I'd lay there on the floor for hours sayin', I hate you mamma, I hate you...I didn't though.

Wicked Games

Paul Boakye

Scene: the United Kingdom

Serio-Comic
Lyn: a woman who has just lost her second baby, 33

> *Following her second miscarriage, Lyn receives a bothersome*
> *phone call from her mother, who seems more interested in*
> *the pending nuptials of Lyn's childhood nemesis than in her*
> *daughter's personal tragedy. Here, Lyn complains of her*
> *mother's lack of sensitivity to her lover, Kofi.*

LYN: Why she has to go on about that Crystal Brown—the bloody
girl! If I hear her name just one more time, I'll hit the roof, I swear
to God—I'll hit the roof.

[KOFI: What was that about?]

LYN: Guess who?

[KOFI: Your mum.]

LYN: How did you guess?

[KOFI: You shouldn't let her get to you like that, Lyn.]

LYN: I can't help it. All my life all that woman's ever done is put me
down. Just because her life is twisted and sad, she has to come
and upset mine. Phoning me to tell me that Crystal's getting married. Well, good for her. I won't be at the wedding. *(She opens
and slams a drawer shut.)* About can't I postpone my holiday or
come back early? I said—no! "Oh, but when you lost the baby
and was in hospital, Crystal was there, though, wasn't she?" I
said, "I didn't tell you to tell Crystal to come. I didn't give you any
message to send out by satellite." She slams the phone down.
Bloody woman! She and that mama-man across the road from
her come like two bloody sisters. Siamese twins, in fact, they
might as well be joined at the hip they're exactly the same—a pair of
gossiping old women! I say to her, "Mum, don't chat my business

to Everett because you know what he's like when he's here—always chatting people's business. Mum, don't chat my business in front of Uncle Everett because you don't know what he's chatting about you behind your back." She says, "Don't be silly, Lyn, darling, chat my business to Uncle Everett?" As soon as uncle, I mean Everett, gets there, chat, chat, chat, chat, chat. And on the subject of his virgin daughter Crystal Brown, well, his tongue never tires. *(She kicks her slippers across the room. He watches her and continues to sharpen the knife. In Everett's voice.)* "B...B...B...B...B...But Ver, remember how when Crystal was going to be a model, how I worked all that overtime at British Telecom, save up money get her top photographer and deportment classes. You remember? I think about those times, you know, Ver, and I think—how on earth could Crystal repay me like this? And It b...b...breaks my heart, believe me, Ver, it b...breaks my heart." I'd like to b...b...b...break his neck! So what if the bloody girl wants to marry a man blacker than the ace of spades? What's it got to do with them? *(She slams a cupboard door, throws off her dressing gown to step into a breezy white dress with buttons down the back.)* Baby, do me up? I know Crystal Brown, and Crystal likes her Blues and she likes her spliff and she likes her big black man like the rest of us. But, oh no, to my mother Crystal Brown is the daughter that she never had, and me, I'm just the unfortunate, unmarried, buckteeth one that somehow turned out far too black for her liking. She likes you though, babes. Must be the international beige. You see how that woman's mind works? Bloody coconut! *(Pause.)* Baby, do you think I'm as good-looking as Crystal Brown?

Yankee Kugel

Judith Silinsky Pasko

Scene: here and now

Serio-Comic
Judith: a young woman handed an extraordinary opportunity, 20s

> *Here, Judith describes how she came to attend the University of Natal in South Africa.*

JUDITH: The Rotary Club. Northridge, California chapter. An all-male bastion of Republican goodwill and back-slapping commerce. The only place in the last twenty years where I was forced to remember the Pledge of Allegiance. I'm thanking them today for…for the *opportunity*—that's a word they love—and the *challenge*—that's another Rotary favorite—of participating in their contest. Turns out every year they offer some lucky college student a fully subsidized scholarship to study anywhere in the world, and it just so happened that while a teacher was reading an announcement about it in class one day, I noticed that absolutely no one was paying attention. Hey, a competition with no competition! That's my kind of competition! So Sally, my debating partner—who had actually been fourth runner-up Michigan Junior Miss—showed me how to finesse my way through an essay; for example, explaining my failing grades all through high school by noting that it, 'took a while to discover my strengths'…as opposed to, 'it took a while to put away my bong.' And then there was my 'statement of intent.' See, I wasn't out to cure cancer here; I just wanted a Dramatic Arts scholarship, but no matter how hard I tried, I couldn't find a philanthropic or even academic spin to put on my less than noble aspiration. So I added a few magic words to my statement to make it appear more noble. I said I would like to study Dramatic Arts so that I could *(Ashamed, but must admit it.)* 'help handicapped children.'

Thank *God* they didn't ask me to explain how an autistic three year old could be helped by a brilliant Antigone! Somehow I survived the weeding-out process, and the competition culminated in an interview with a cadre of ancient Rotarians. In an avocado green, mildew-scented conference room in a San Fernando Valley bowling alley, I fielded such weighty questions as, 'How would you entertain a group of foreigners in an American way?' *(Obviously baffled.)* I dunno…crack pipe and a blow job? I've got it! I'd have an All American Barbecue! Now that was a great answer! I went on and on, describing everything from the red-checkered tablecloths to the baby back ribs to the Dixieland band I'd have playing in the background. Just then I was interrupted by the lone Black Rotarian who asked, 'Where exactly is Dixie?' *(Pause.)* I'm pretty sure it was that moment which led to this moment: standing here, thanking these nice men for: Second Place. You see, geography was never my strong suit. Australia and Austria blurred in my brain for years, so Dixie might as well have been the land where paper cups were made. Whatever it was I managed to mumble was clearly unimpressive, because here I am: offering a warm congratulations to Maria, the Rotary Scholarship winner, who is off to study Microbiology in Argentina. She speaks fluent Spanish. *(Pause, then, so sweetly, waving good-bye.)* Chinga tu Madre, Maria! But just then, rickety old Mr. Bensen informs me that there is a second place prize! Now we're talking! Let's see: First Place winner gets a fully subsidized scholarship, a round trip ticket, and money for food, lodging, supplies and travel, and Second Place winner gets: a ruler. *(Pause, then a big smile.)* Thank you so much for the lovely ruler! I know exactly how I'd like to use it! *(Lights down. The podium returns to switchboard status and she is back behind the desk, headset on, scribbling furiously. Lights up.)* So the question is, why, two years after I became the proud winner of a Rotary ruler, am I getting a call at work from some Rotarian? They must want me to make a speech. That's it: They got a last minute cancellation from their 'Guns Are People Too,' guest speaker and they're combing their very old Rolodex looking for a replacement. *(She punches a console button then listens, incredulous.)* Now, let me see if I've got this straight: You've been going through your files, and it turns out that Maria never went to Argentina? Why? *(Pause.)* I guess that is 'none of my concern.' And since I was the second place winner, the scholarship is now *mine?* Is this some sort of Vanessa Williams thing? I managed to finally graduate from college over two years ago, and— *(Rethinking her approach.)* —can Graduate students use the scholarship? *(Pause.)* Even if they're not actually in Graduate School? *(Pause.)* Even if they haven't been near a campus in two years? *(Pause.)* Really? *(Extremely suspicious.)* Something's wrong, this is too weird, it's a trick, it's gotta be, I mean this is just too...bizarre. *What's the catch? (She hangs up, shrugging.)* They send me a form to fill out. 'List three schools that you would like to attend' anywhere in the world...that I can speak the language fluently. Unfortunately, since I am mono-linguistic, about nine-tenths of the world is offlimits. *Merde.* So I make a list of all the English-speaking countries and their pros and cons: Australia. Wait, don't they speak Australian? Isn't that where Freud was born? Oh, never mind. Scotland. *(Dreamily.)* Heather...bagpipes... *(Then.)* haggis. *(She shudders.)* Canada! But that doesn't count as a year abroad; it's attached. That's like going to the prom with your cousin. Oh, this is silly! There's only one place for me to go: England, my England! This lump, this sod, this clot of land! Home of Shakespeare! Olivier! Benny Hill! *(She picks up a pen and fills in the form.)* I've got to go to England. I'll write down three schools, and whichever one they pick, I'll go! *(She looks at the form closely.)* What's this? An asterisk? *(Ominous chords play briefly.)* Beware the ass to risk: it may be your own. This, I learn in hindsight. At the time, I did what everyone does: ignored it. It probably said, 'Batteries not included,' or, 'actual mileage may vary.' So I blithely went on my way, bragging to all I encountered that this time next year I would be studying the thee-ah-tah in England. More letters came: checklists, passport and visa information, and suddenly, *it was real!* I was *really* going abroad! Finally, *the* letter came: the one that instructed me to call up Rotary International to learn which school in Jolly Old England would have the honor of my attendance. Mind you, I still have my rewarding career as a receptionist, so this must be done in an empty office at lunchtime. *(She punches some numbers that she reads off a letter.)* A cheerful voice informs me I'll be studying at: The University of Natal. I heard, 'Nepal,' as in India. The Union Carbide accident had just blinded thousands of people, and now I was about to join them? "Excuse me, but where is that?" A pause; a shuffling of papers. "The University of Natal is in Durban." Turban? I *am* going to India! I'll be stumbling around India, blind, wearing a turban! By now I have been told the name of the University, and the city that it's in, and I still have no idea where I'm going! And where is that? South America? *What?* I can't even speak Spanish, except cuss words! What—oh, South *Africa. (Lights out. Then, in darkness, after a pause.)* You're kidding, right? *(A spotlight shines on her frightened face.)* The asterisk! *(She frantically searches the desk for the form, then reads aloud.)* "In the event that the country you choose has an overabundance of Rotary Scholars, a school will be chosen for you in a country with fewer scholarship recipients." *(She slams the form on the desk.)* Of *course* there's a shortage of students in— *(She refers to the form.)* "Durban." *Who the hell wants to go to South Africa?* Here's my life: Five minutes ago I was standing at the threshold of my bright, limitless future, and now I am the punch line of a cosmic joke. Durban is in the province of Natal, and the violent uprisings and bombings that are a daily occurrence often wind up on the cover of *Time* and *Newsweek* and, frankly scare the shit out of me. I don't get it. Do they send students to Beirut? Uganda? It's also extremely fashionable to hate South Africa all of a sudden, and why not? Their government segregates and denies political power to seventy-two percent of the population. Minority Whites rule, and treat the Blacks—well, like we did before the Civil War. *(She heads back to the desk, sits, and begins to write.)* I compose a letter, indicating with what I hope is the perfect combination of gratitude and groveling, that I'm extremely grateful for the challenge, but given the—how shall I put it—recent escalation of violence, it might be…what's the word?—inopportune for me to get my white ass *blown up in a shopping mall!* I'm so ambivalent that I poll my friends to help me decide. Steve was most enthusiastic. "You'll be like Christopher Isherwood in pre-Hitler Berlin! You'll observe the people, write *Durban Stories,* and win the Pulitzer Prize!" That's Steve. But they were unanimous. Their view seemed to be: You got called two years after you won second place, and they're sending you a round trip ticket and all expenses paid—I think Paul put it most succinctly when he said, and I quote, "What are you, fuckin' nuts?" They're right, my pals; someone or something seemed to be going to an awful lot of trouble to send me to this place called Durban. It didn't seem right to say, 'No thanks, I'm scared.' Besides, there had to be a little bit of the revolutionary in me; after all, my mother was Another Mother for Peace! We even had the poster on the wall of the family room, "War is not healthy for children and other living things." I could be more than Christopher Isherwood passively watching a decaying country! I could be a *force!* I could personally help turn the tide and end apart-tide. Apart-aid. *(Pause.)* I should learn how to pronounce it first.

Women's 1996 Permissions

The Adjustment by Michael T. Folie. Copyright © 1996 by Michael T. Folie. Reprinted by permission of The Graham Agency All Inquiries: Earl Graham, The Graham Agency, 311 West 43rd Street, New York, NY 10036

Alphabet Of Flowers by Elyse Nass. Copyright © 1993 by Elyse Nass. Reprinted by permission of the author. All Inquiries: Elyse Nass, 5915 47th Avenue, Woodside, NY 11377

Ask Nostradamus by R. J. Marx. Copyright © 1996 by R. J. Marx. Preprinted by permission of the author. Inquiries: R.J. Marx, 31 Ridge Road, Katonah, NY 10536, (914) 232-6781

The Batting Cage by Joan Ackermann. Copyright ©. Professionals and amateurs are hereby warned that *The Batting Cage* by Joan Ackermann is subject to a royalty. It is fully protected by the copyright laws of the United States of America and of all countries covered by the International Copyright Union (Including the Dominion of Canada and the rest of the British Commonwealth), and of all countries with which the United States has reciprocal copyright relations. All rights, including professional, amateur, motion picture, recitataion, lecturing, public reading, radio broadcasting, television, video or sound taping, all other forms of mechanical or electronic reproductions such as information storage and retrieval systems and photocopying and the rights of translation into foreign languages, are strictly reserved. All inquiries should be addressed to Mary Harden at: Harden-Curtis Associates, 850 Seventh Avenue, Suite 405, New York, NY 10019

Burning Down The House by Jocelyn Beard. Copyright © 1996 by Jocelyn Beard, all rights reserved. Reprinted by permission of the author. Inquiries: J. Beard, RR#2 Box 151, Patterson, NY 12563, kitowski@computer.net

The Church Of The Holy Ghost by Ludmilla Bollow. Copyright © 1995 by Ludmilla Bollow. Reprinted by permission of author: Ludmilla Bollow and Publisher: Broadway Play Publishing. The complete play may be obtained from: Broadway Play Publishing 56 E. 81st Street, New York, NY 10028. Inquiries: Ludmilla Bollow, 314 W. Sugar Lane, Milwaukee, WI 53217

Dance With Me by Stephen Temperley. Copyright © 1996 by Stephen

Smith and Kraus *Books For Actors*
THE MONOLOGUE SERIES

SCENE STUDY SERIES

YOUNG ACTOR SERIES

If you require pre-publication information about upcoming Smith and Kraus books, you may receive our semi-annual catalogue, free of charge, by sending your name and address to *Smith and Kraus Catalogue, P.O. Box 127, Lyme, NH 03768. Or call us at (603) 922-5118, fax (603) 922-3348.*